TWAYNE'S WORLD AUTHORS SERIES

A Survey of the World's Literature

Sylvia E. Bowman, Indiana University

GENERAL EDITOR

SPAIN

Gerald Wade, Vanderbilt University

EDITOR

Ramón Pérez de Ayala

(TWAS 138)

TWAYNE'S WORLD AUTHORS SERIES (TWAS)

*The purpose of TWAS is to survey the major writers
—novelists, dramatists, historians, poets, philosophers,
and critics—of the nations of the world. Among the
national literatures. covered are those of Australia,
Canada, China, Eastern Europe, France, Germany,
Greece, Italy, Japan, Latin America, New Zealand,
Poland, Russia, Scandinavia, Spain, and the African
nations, as well as Hebrew, Yiddish, and Latin Classical literature. This survey is complemented by
Twayne's United States Authors Series and
English Authors Series.*

*The intent of each volume in these series is to
present a critical-analytical study of the works of the
writer; to include biographical and historical material
that may be necessary for understanding, appreciation, and critical appraisal of the writer; and to
present all material in clear, concise English—but not
to vitiate the scholarly content of the work
by doing so.*

Ramón Pérez de Ayala

By MARGUERITE C. RAND

University of Maryland

Twayne Publishers, Inc.　::　New York

To my husband,
Colonel Oscar Ripley Rand,
United States Army, Retired,
with deepest appreciation
for his constant understanding,
encouragement, and cooperation.

Acknowledgments

I wish to express my deep appreciation to Señora Mabel Rick de Pérez de Ayala, widow of the distinguished writer, for her gracious hospitality and the valuable and interesting information which I received from her, in my visits to her home in Madrid. I also thank Señor J. García Mercadal, editor of the *Obras completas* of Pérez de Ayala, for his kindly assistance and information.

My sincere gratitude goes also to my friends and colleagues at the University of Maryland: Mrs. Marion Ament, Mrs. Joan Tarwater, and Dr. Marie Panico, and to Dr. Pilar Sáenz of American University, all of whom made helpful commentaries and assisted me in finding elusive information. I am especially grateful to Dr. Graciela P. Nemes who read the entire manuscript and gave me valuable suggestions.

I thank Professor Gerald E. Wade for his prompt and helpful cooperation, editorial comments, and encouragement in the preparation of this study.

Finally, I am grateful to the General Research Board of the University of Maryland for a Faculty Research Award, which assisted me greatly in the completion of this work.

Contents

Preface

THE purpose of this study is to acquaint the reader with the works of one of Spain's great literary figures of the twentieth century, Ramón Pérez de Ayala (1880-1962), poet, novelist, essayist, and diplomat. We have discussed his works by genres and in chronological order, when possible. Most of his major works are dated, but many of his more than nine thousand essays bear no date or place of publication. At the end of each chapter of this study, we have tried to indicate the salient points in the genre studied.

We have gone rather extensively into the contents of his individual works, so that his writings may speak for themselves, and the reader may better understand the comments on them. Any translations which we have made are our own, unless otherwise indicated, and at times we have limited ourselves to paraphrasing the text. While we have read many studies on Pérez de Ayala, both in the United States and Spain, we have not quoted extensively from the critics, as we have preferred to make our own judgments insofar as possible, although probably influenced at times by critics whom we name and to whom we express our appreciation. In our Bibliography of Secondary Sources we have included only those studies which we believe to be most helpful to the reader. We have restricted the Chronology to the most important events in Ayala's life and to his outstanding publications; further details will be found in the text.

Pérez de Ayala was born in his beloved Asturias in northern Spain, and lived not only in Spain, but in a number of foreign countries, such as Italy, Germany, France, and England. Here he represented the Second Spanish Republic as Spanish Ambassador to Great Britain (1931-1936). After the electoral triumph of the leftist Frente Popular, he resigned his post in 1936. He believed in democratic principles but was never a radical in his political thought and actions. He spent some months in the United States on two occasions and lived for some years in Buenos Aires. He and his family returned to Spain in 1954, where he lived until his death.

Ayala's sound humanistic training, his travels, and his widely varied experiences have made of him a man of great breadth of culture, outlook, and comprehension. He has been accused of being too intellectual and philosophical in his works, but his writings also show humor, irony, perspective and contrast, and have a wealth of human content.

As a philosopher and poet, he seeks Beauty, Truth, and Good. Fundamental Christian principles are basic to his character. He seeks to understand man and the world with his keenly perceptive mind, but he does not wish to pass judgment. He believes in tolerance and comprehension, and his ideal is to do his part toward bringing harmony to the Universe. He is a universal writer, humanistic and human, who loved old wines, old books, and old friends. He was also a devoted husband, father, and grandfather.

MARGUERITE C. RAND

Washington, D. C.

Chronology

1880   August 9: Ramón Pérez de Ayala born in Oviedo, Asturias.

1888-   Student in Jesuit College of San Zoil in Carñión de los
1890   Condes.

1890-   Student in Jesuit College of the Immaculate Conception
1894   in Gijón where he acquired the foundation of a sound
        humanistic education, reflected in his later writings.

1896-   Completed full course in Law at the University of Oviedo,
1902   then called the Athens of Spain because of the University's
        distinguished faculty.

1902   Went to Madrid to study for doctorate in Law and made
        friendships with many of the outstanding literary figures of
        the day.

1903   Published first book of poetry, *La paz del sendero (The
        Peaceful Path)*, highly eulogized by Rubén Darío.

1903-   Collaborator with Juan Ramón Jiménez in *Helios,* con-
1904   tributing poetry, short stories, and literary criticism.

1907   Published first novel, *Tinieblas en las cumbres (Darkness
        on the Heights)*, with the pseudonym Plotino Cuevas.
        April to December in London, writing articles for *El
        Imparcial* in Madrid. In December suicide of father, be-
        lieving himself ruined by friends whom he had trusted,
        caused Ayala's immediate return to Spain.

1910   Published novel *A.M.D.G. (To the Greater Glory of God)*,
        based on experiences in the Jesuit school in Gijón.

1911   In fall went to Florence to study art. Met young American,
        Miss Mabel Rick, who was later to become his wife, and
        who was studying music. That fall, Ayala wrote his third
        novel, *La pata de la raposa (The Fox's Paw)*, published
        in 1912.

1912   In fall Miss Rick returned to the United States, and

Ayala went to Germany, where he completed his fourth novel.

1913   Published fourth novel, *Troteras y danzaderas (Mummers and Dancers)*. First trip to the United States. Married Miss Mabel Rick on September first, in Allentown, Pennsylvania. While in the United States, Ayala wrote numerous articles for Madrid newspapers. Couple returned to Spain in late fall.

1914   Birth of first son, Juan, in late fall.

1916   Published his three poematic novels of Spanish life: *Prometeo (Prometheus); Luz de Domingo (Sunday Sunlight), La caída de los Limones (The Fall of the House of Limón)*. Also published volume of poetry, *El sendero innumerable (The Path of Infinite Variations)*. Wrote various articles on the tragedy of World War I. Sent to the Italian front as war correspondent for *La Prensa* of Buenos Aires.

1917   Published *Hermann, encadenado (Hermann, in Chains)*, volume of articles previously sent to *La Prensa*. First volume of *Las máscaras (The Masks)*, theatrical criticism.

1918   Published *Política y toros (Politics and Bulls)*. Birth of second son, Eduardo, in April.

1919   Published second volume of *Las Máscaras*.

1919- Second trip to the United States, where he wrote articles
1920   for Madrid newspapers.

1921   Published third volume of poetry, *El sendero andante (The Flowing Path)*; also a major novel, *Belarmino y Apolonio*.

1922   Received journalistic prize, "Mariano de Cavia," for two articles on Ignacio Zuloaga, in *El Liberal*, December 1, 2, 1921.

1923   Published two-part major novel, *Luna de miel, Luna de hiel (Honeymoon, Bitter Moon)* and its continuation *Los trabajos de Urbano y Simona (The Labors of Urbano and Simona)*.

1924   Publication of two collections of short novels: *El ombligo del mundo (The Umbilical Center of the World)*, and *Bajo el signo de Artemisa (Under the Sign of Artemisa)*.

1926   Publication of last major novel, *Tigre Juan (Tiger Juan)*, and its continuation, *El curandero de su honra (The*

Healer of his Honor), for which Ayala received the first National Prize for Literature.

1928   Published last known fiction, a short novel, *Justicia (Justice).* Elected member of the Royal Spanish Academy. Never made his inaugural address and died member-elect.

1931   Great political unrest in Spain. Abandonment of throne by Alfonso XIII. Pérez de Ayala joined the intellectuals, Ortega y Gasset and Marañón, in forming a "League for the Defense of the Republic." Second Spanish Republic proclaimed in April. Pérez de Ayala was named to represent it as Ambassador to Great Britain.

1931-   Years as Spanish Ambassador in London. Further serious
1936   political disturbances in Spain caused him to resign his post in the spring of 1936. Received honorary doctorate from University of London. Returned briefly to Madrid in summer of 1936.

1936-   Spanish Civil War. Pérez de Ayala and his wife spent
1939   these years in Biarritz and Paris, returning to Spain at the close of the Civil War.

1940   Ayala invited to lecture in various countries of South America and took residence in Buenos Aires, where he continued his journalistic writing.

1949   Spanish Society of New York conferred its medal on Pérez de Ayala, Juan Ramón Jiménez, and Ortega y Gasset. Ayala made brief trip to Spain and France. Returned to Buenos Aires without making his promised inaugural address for reception into the Royal Spanish Academy.

1954   Death of older son, Juan. Ayala's final return to Madrid, where he continued to write for newspapers, principally *ABC,* until shortly before his death. These essays and some earlier writings have been collected by J. García Mercadal and published in some dozen volumes, several of them posthumously. We shall not list them here as they are all included in our Bibliography, and most of them discussed in our text.

1957   Publication of Ayala's *Obras selectas (Select Works).*
1960   Received the Juan March Prize for Creative Writing.
1962   August 5: Died in Madrid, leaving widow, one son, and various grandchildren.
1969   May, widow died.

CHAPTER 1

Formative Years

IN his volume of essays, *Amistades y recuerdos (Friendships and Recollections)*, 1961,[1] Ramón Pérez de Ayala writes of the talent, genius and fame of an author, remarking that literary fame and glory are dependent not only upon the genius of the writer himself, but also upon the circumstances that surround him, the environmental atmosphere, and the historical moment, recalling, of course, Taine's *race, milieu et moment*. Ayala cannot conceive of Alexander without the power of Macedonia, nor Caesar without Rome and her legions.

It would be difficult, also, to conceive of Pérez de Ayala without his native Asturias, which forms the background of much of his writing, or of the unrest which marked the history of Spain and of Europe during many of Ayala's eighty-two years, affecting his life and outlook. However, Pérez de Ayala cannot be considered a regional writer, nor to any great extent a political writer. The message and spirit of his works far transcend such limitations. He sought to comprehend the world about him with love, and to contribute to its harmony. He did not try to judge, but to understand. Ayala wrote in 1913: "The comprehension of the universe through love has its ramifications in four kinds of love: the love of things, the love of children, the love of women, and the love of God."[2]

His thought closely parallels that of his friend and contemporary, José Ortega y Gasset, who, in his *Meditaciones del Quijote*, wrote an opening essay addressed to the reader, declaring that there flows beneath the surface of his essays, "a doctrine of love." Here we find his famous statement: "I am I and my circumstance, and if I do not save it, I do not save myself." Ortega clarifies his meaning. "One must seek the meaning of that which surrounds him," for "this surrounding circumstance

forms the other half of one's person." For Ortega as for Ayala,
perspective is important, and the intuition of superior values
enriches our contact with smaller ones. Love toward the nearby
and the insignificant gives us "a consciousness and comprehension
of the sublime." Further, "man renders the maximum of his
capacity when he acquires the full consciousness of the circumstances about him. Through them he communicates with the
universe."[3] Ayala has a similar doctrine as he seeks with love
the significance of his surroundings, first of all of his native
Asturias.

I *Asturian Background*

Asturias is frequently called the Switzerland of Spain. Ayala
finds it incomparably beautiful in his description in an early
essay, "Asturian Pantheism" (1903). He writes with love of his
region's "gigantic peaks, of live rock and chimerical forms, that
scale the sky like Titans," the "grave blue mountains, capped
with snow . . . ' dreaming in the distance," "the charming
Virgilian valleys," the "meadows of perennial green, bordered
by poplars, oaks, and chestnut trees," "the age-old forests, filled
with religious abstraction, legend, enchantment." There is the
fragrance of honeysuckle and the soft music of cattle bells and
melancholy country songs. In this "dreamy atmosphere," the
people "are animated by a spirit of their own, conscious and
divine." Even the animals reflect their surroundings. The cows
appear "resigned and sad, judicious and thoughtful." The dogs
"bark dreamily without deigning to look at the passerby, or they
howl at night, scenting death." The atmosphere reflects a "deep
feeling of pantheistic pessimism, romantic, as opposed to the
classic serenity of the South."[4]

Modern Spain has its origin in Asturias, for there, in 718, at
Covadonga, was fought the first battle of the Christian Recon-
quest, after the invasion by the Moors, in 711. Asturias has
resisted many would-be invaders of its mountain fastnesses.
Their motto is "Asturias never conquered." There is a strong
feeling of independence among the Asturians. (*OC*, I, 1097)

II *Family Background*

Ramón Pérez de Ayala was born in Asturias, in the city of
Oviedo, on the ninth of August, 1880,[5] the second of three

children. His brother Cirilo was four years older, and his sister Asunción was somewhat younger than he. All three are now dead. The young Ramón was very devoted to his parents, as is evident from various references to them in his poetry and some of his essays.

His father was from Valdenebro, in Tierra de Campos, near Palencia, and the author refers to him as of pure Castilian stock. The senior Pérez de Ayala, Don Cirilo, possessed of a spirit of adventure, decided to go to Asturias to establish a business, and there met a charming young lady who was later to be his wife. Meanwhile, he decided that Asturias was too limited a field for his ambitions, and he departed for Cuba. This also seemed to prove unsatisfactory, or perhaps he felt a nostalgia for his sweetheart and his native land. In any event, within three months he returned to Asturias to engage in business, and he married his beloved Carmen Fernández del Portal, a native of Gijón. Thus Ramón Pérez de Ayala had a Castilian father and an Asturian mother.

His biographer, Francisco Agustín, refers to his father as a Goth and to the mother as a Celt, and feels that the son inherited specific qualities from each. As a good Castilian he was never in a hurry, and was a firm defender of his beliefs. A Gothic trait was his adhesion to general and disinterested ideas. His Celtic trait was his poetic imagination. He was "very Asturian . . . very Spanish, and very European. . . . penetrating, intuitive, universal, subtle, conscientious, talented, . . . and a humorist."[6] Impressed by the admirable characters of his parents, he wanted to be like them.

III *Early Education*

One of Ayala's earliest memories is that of his first teacher, Don Juan Rodríguez Muñiz, whom he recalls affectionately, many years later, in an essay for *ABC* (Nov. 23, 1960). (*Amistades,* p. 135) The patient and kindly Don Juan had a private school attended by some one hundred children, in Oviedo. Pérez de Ayala writes that Don Juan was the first person outside his home that inspired in him respect and love. In this school he learned painstakingly to write. On Saturdays, the good Don Juan taught the boys the Holy Scripture, and throughout his life Pérez de Ayala retained the images of figures of the Old

Testament described by Don Juan. This was undoubtedly an early inspiration that caused Pérez de Ayala to be an avid and constant reader of the Bible over the years. When we visited his widow in their Madrid home in 1966, she showed us his copies of the Bible in Greek, Latin, and English, on a shelf within easy reach in his living room, and which were part of his daily reading. Pérez de Ayala wrote that this first teacher also inspired in him a desire to partake of the fruits of knowledge.

At the age of eight, Ramón was taken to a Jesuit school of San Zoil, in Carrión de los Condes, near Palencia, where he was the youngest of some two hundred students. Here he suffered loneliness, far from home, from familiar landscapes and family faces. Above all, he missed his mother, especially on retiring to his room which seemed to him a little white sepulcher. He was consoled by Father Julio Cejador, who visited him in the evenings, bringing him caramels, and placing his hand on the child's brow in an effort to dispel his sorrows.

Cejador, philologist and literary historian, was kind to the child, and later, when he withdrew from the Jesuit Order, he spent some time in the home of the parents of the young Ramón, where he exercised some influence on the child. According to Francisco Agustín, Cejador not only taught Greek, but he played the piano and read the mystics. The two enjoyed various cultural activities. The young Ramón, already much interested in modern poetry, introduced to his professor the poetry of the great Nicaraguan Rubén Darío, and called his attention to the ingenious Asturian poetry, revealing a surprising power of observation. (Agustín, pp. 16-17) Pérez de Ayala began his career as a poet at a very early age. He declared in an interview with Julio Trenas, some years ago, that he was writing verses in the Jesuit school at the age of eight.[7]

After spending two years in San Zoil, Ramón entered the Jesuit school of the Immaculate Conception in Gijón, in 1890. His experiences in this school are described in the novel *A. M. D. G. (To the Greater glory of God, Ad majorem Dei Gloriam)*—the motto of the Jesuits. Here was cultivated his dialectical capacity, which he later used in his criticism of the Jesuits. He suffered physical punishments in the school, and, as Agustín points out, "what is worse, he breathed an atmosphere of moral and religious hypocrisy which threatened to destroy his personality." (p. 17)

He was a very precocious student who accepted for his thinking only what he judged worthy of acceptance. He was called the "anarchist." He wanted to be the leader, and he became so.

It was here that he first, as a young student, met the well-known sculptor, Sebastián Miranda. Miranda has told us that he was first attracted by Ramón's impressive voice, and that he was even more impressed by what the young boy had to say, thus revealing the younger student's regard for him. Sebastián Miranda and Pérez Ayala were lifelong friends.

Despite the adversities of his four years in this school (1890-1894), Ramón acquired the basis of a solid humanistic education. He achieved an excellent knowledge of Greek and Latin, and he was an assiduous reader of classical literature. Ayala later declared that he was a formidable Latinist at the age of eleven.

In the year of 1891 he met an Englishman, Mr. Walsh, who had come to direct an iron foundry in the vicinity of the Ayala family's country home near Gijón, where they spent their summer vacations. This Englishman took an interest in the boy and promised to send him a book from London, so that he might learn English. On returning to school in September, he received the book, which had for him not only a practical but also a symbolic value. It was for him like "a little window" through which he first looked out at the world. He had been taught that "Spain was the umbilical center of the world," and that of this, "the Company of Jesus was the geometric center." Thanks to this little book, the young Ramón felt "a powerful longing to be a man, an ardent desire for inextinguishable integrity and perfection, understanding that one cannot be a Spaniard nor a good patriot of his great fatherland without being first a man of truth, a man of value to other men, wherever chance may have placed him, here or there, in his native land or in the most distant latitude."[8]

Years later, in September, 1936, Pérez de Ayala, finding it necessary to leave Spain because of the Civil War, had to abandon all of his possessions including the gift from Mr. Walsh. He commented later: "But all that which that book engendered I bear within me. That modest little book has perhaps influenced the course of my later life as much or more than all the learned books with which I was then to indoctrinate or entertain myself."[9]

IV *Years at the University of Oviedo*

After four years at the Jesuit school in Gijón, years that seemed

to the youth to pass with incredible slowness, he went on to
the University of Oviedo. In an interview with Riopérez y Milá,
Ayala refers to his youthful desire to study Industrial Engineering,
but for this he would have had to go to Bilbao or Barcelona.
His mother was not willing for her son, at the age of fourteen, to
go so far away and live alone in a large city. Therefore, it was
decided that he should remain at home and attend the University
of Oviedo.[10] Here, according to the author's own statement, he
studied two years in the Faculty of Sciences and then completed
the full course in Law. (*Tributo*, p. 275)

Despite the relatively small number of students in the University, Oviedo was called in this period the Athens of Spain
because of the superior quality of its faculty. Among Ayala's
professors were the outstanding novelist and critic, Leopoldo
Alas ("Clarín"); the distinguished historian, Rafael Altamira;
Melquíades Alvarez, professor of Roman Law; and others of
importance. Ayala has written of them in various essays, stressing
the European accent and the Renaissance atmosphere which they
brought to the University. (*OC*, I, 1153-61) Pérez de Ayala was
especially devoted to "Clarín," and one of the young writer's first
journalistic publications, "El maestro," was dedicated to this
much loved professor and published in *El Imparcial* of Madrid
in 1904. (*OC*, I, XVII-XX)

Francisco Agustín comments that the young Ayala was not "a
model student. However, his most intelligent professors appreciated him extraordinarily, especially . . . 'Clarín' . . . Ayala
utilized his spiritual faculties in devoted service to Art and
Literature. He read a great deal and sketched." (Agustín, p. 18)

V *Artistic Interests*

From youth, Ayala was interested in art. He mentions having
had a drawing teacher at home, at the age of fourteen. (*OC*, I,
xvii) Agustín refers to Ayala as being not only a writer, but also
a sketcher and painter, and comments that he had learned from
Sebastián Miranda, who had made a bust of Ayala, that "the
first model in clay was done in collaboration with Ayala. Together they experienced the delightful aesthetic wonder of joining
line and light to a human and expressive purpose." During our
conversation in Madrid, Miranda confirmed this fact.

Ayala's interest in art was to give him solace during the rest of his life. Over the years, he filled his home with objects of art such as paintings by Murillo and Sánchez Coello, portraits of Ayala by Sorolla, Vázquez Díaz, Zuloaga, Eduardo Chicharro, bronze busts by Julio Antonio and by Juan Cristóbal, to mention a few. There are sculptures by Sebastían Miranda of Ayala's younger son, Eduardo, and of the widow of his older son, Juan, and a portrait of the poet's widow by the Cordoban artist, Adsuara. Ayala studied art in Florence, Italy (1911-1912). Of special interest to us, as we saw them in his home, were three beautiful watercolors done by him in Argentina.

His interest in art is further revealed in various essays and monographs concerning numerous painters and sculptors. Zuloaga was his friend for many years, and for his essay on Zuloaga, published in *El Liberal* (1922), he was awarded the "Mariano de Cavia" prize. His artistic talent is evident, also, in his writings, particularly in the delicate variations of color, and the plastic effects in his landscapes.

VI *Early Years in Madrid*

After completing his courses in Law at the University of Oviedo, he went to Madrid, probably in 1902, to study for his doctorate in Law at the University of Madrid. We have found no evidence as to whether he completed the doctorate. He was beginning to feel the compelling attractions of a literary career.

There is little doubt that another purpose in his going to Madrid was to become acquainted with the literary world of the capital. Among his friends in Madrid were the most outstanding figures of the period: José Ortega Munilla, director of the important newspaper, *El Imparcial* and his famous son, José Ortega y Gasset; the two great Galician writers, Valle-Inclán and Pardo Bazán; the outstanding novelist of the nineteenth century, Pérez Galdós; the prolific Basque novelist, Pío Baroja; the Nicaraguan poet, Rubén Darío; the great master of style in novel and essay, Azorín (José Martínez Ruiz); the later Nobel prize-winning poet, Juan Ramón Jiménez, and many others.

After Pérez de Ayala had visited Juan Ramón Jiménez, in Madrid, the latter described him in a letter to Rubén Darío as "a poet of considerable talent and a great deal of culture."[11]

Ayala was indeed a man of great culture. Although young in years, he had not spent his time in vain. He was always a prolific reader, a master of the Greek and Latin classics, with a considerable knowledge also of Spanish and other European literatures. Besides his native Spanish and his Greek and Latin, he spoke French, German, Italian, Portuguese, and English. He was modest about his achievements. He once remarked humorously that men speak many languages, "so that they can make foolish remarks in one more language."

During this period in Madrid, Ayala was learning much from the life about him, and much from his important literary contacts. He was also doing considerable writing, particularly in the field of poetry. He felt his literary vocation ever more deeply.

The historical moment was also significant. Spain, in the early twentieth century was trying to recover from the shock of her defeat in 1898 by the United States, and the loss of the last part of her one-time great colonial empire. There was a marked unrest and dissatisfaction among the leading thinkers and writers—many of those prominent associates of Ayala. The well-known "Generation of 1898," whose most outstanding writers were Azorín, Unamuno, Baroja, Antonio Machado, and later, Valle-Inclán, were dissatisfied with the Spanish present. They sought the true reality of Spain and a revival of that latent spirit which had made Spain great in the past. They did not seek greatness in a material sense. They strove for an intellectual, spiritual, and literary Renaissance. A reflection of this attitude is found in the writings of Ayala, particularly in his early works.

CHAPTER 2

Pérez de Ayala, the Poet

A LTHOUGH Pérez de Ayala is probably best known for his novels, there is no doubt of his great love for poetry, a vital part of his literary production. We have already noted his declaration that he wrote his first poem at the age of eight. His three published volumes of poetry are quite well known: *La paz del sendero (The Peaceful Path)*, 1903; *El sendero innumerable (The Path of Infinite Variations)*, 1916; *El sendero andante (The Flowing Path)*, 1921.

About the time of the publication of the first volume, he was also collaborating with Juan Ramón Jiménez and several other prominent literary figures in *Helios*, a literary monthly that appeared from April, 1903, to the spring of 1904. Its title derived, undoubtedly, from the name of the ancient Greek god, Helios, charioteer of the sun, shedding its light upon the earth. In this review, Ayala published poems, several short stories, a brief bit of theater, and some literary criticism. In an article on "Poesía" ("Poetry"), *Helios*, VI, Sept. 1903, he remarks that, despite the gloomy forecast of some prophets of an early disappearance of the poetic form, he can foresee "the luminous dawn of a Renaissance in poetry." His novels, early and late, are interspersed with poetry.

I *Ayala's Ideas on Poetry*

For the first edition of his *Poesías completas (Complete Poems)*, Buenos Aires, 1942, the author wrote a significant Introduction, "Alegato 'Pro Domo Mea,'" or "Allegation in Support of My Poetic Labyrinth." We may recall that Virgil used "Domo" in the sense of a labyrinth or sacred grotto. Ayala feels that "the good poet is born, not made," and that "one writes verses through a natural necessity, he can do no less." Poetry is "not one's daily bread," but "true poetry is born of an involuntary and not a deliberate exaltation, which coincides with certain moments or periods of tonic accent in one's individual life." (*OC*, II, 78).

Ayala also explains his reasons for his use of poetry in his novels: that "poetry is the point of reference, and we might say the atmosphere in profundity of narrative prose." At times, "the character in the novel goes through critical moments of psychically complex tension and subtlety, which are in themselves ineffable, like the intuitions of the mystics." To express these, "the novelist can only resort to poetry." (*OC* II, 78, 79)

Here, also, we find Ayala's projected plan for his volumes of poetry in which he wished to express poetically man's pathway through life. He explains: "The cosmos has its four elements. The year and the life of man have their four seasons and their four ages. Adolescence is the age of nutrition and growth on the native soil, as the tree grows through its roots; it bears with it flower, aroma, and warbling. Youth is the age of exploration and adventures, an age seduced by the sea with its lascivious fluctuations and the song of its ambiguous sirens. Maturity is the age of honesty and purification, when the fire of life burns, more compressed, strong, and tenacious, through whose action the dross is eliminated, and there remains the clean gold; perhaps only a pure silver ash." (*OC*, II, 79-80)

Ayala wrote poems regarding these first three ages of man, although the collection of poems concerning maturity, *El sendero ardiente (The Fiery Path)*, published for the first time in his *Obras completas,* Vol. II, is incomplete. The poems regarding old age were apparently never written, although he had explained his ideas for them: "Old age is the age of contemplation; a stoic farewell in the antechamber of the final transition; it is, or should be, crystalline like the high heaven. In the winter of the year and of life, . . . man recapitulates his works and his days, in a transcendental balancing of accounts, and finds out if the year and the life have been dissipated in vain; or, on the contrary, he can present himself before the tribunal of God, saying with reverence: 'Lord, I have not gone through time like an arrow, sterile or noxious, in the darkness of the night!" (*OC*, II, 80)

Pérez de Ayala believed that "each age demands its poetry." "Poetry deals with elemental subjects and is moreover, a participation in, or a glimpse of the cosmic conscience; . . . its eternal themes are God, Love, and Death." (*OC*, II, 80)

II Primeros frutos (First Fruits)

In the poet's *Obras Completas*, Vol. II (1965), we find a far more complete collection of his poems than elsewhere. The editor, J. García Mercadal, has gathered a group of some fifty poems under the title *Primeros frutos (First Fruits)*, many of them hitherto unpublished, and many of them undated. The few dates that appear range from 1903 to 1922, thus covering a rather extensive period.

The first poems of this collection are called "Sonetos en el gusto francés," or "Sonnets in the French Taste," with a subtitle, "Redondelas a la manera de Carlos Orleáns, príncipe y poeta" ("Roundelays in the Manner of Charles of Orleans, Prince and Poet"). It was Charles who held his court of artists and poets at Blois on the banks of the Loire in the fifteenth century, and who wrote sonnets and roundelays on such subjects as nature, love, and death, generally regarded as having greater value for their beauty of form than for their depth of content.

These poems of Ayala, which appeared originally in *Helios* (1903), are a type of sonnet written in two stanzas of eight and six lines respectively, repeating concepts and consonantal rhymes in harmony with the theme of love, personified in various beloved women and their individual attractions. One is "golden light, a light sent by God when the day is dying"; another, "the fragile figure of a pre-Raphaelic painting"; another, the poet would like to immortalize in a Byzantine "icon of alabaster and silver." All appear to be lost loves of his youth, recalled with melancholy. There are many more poems in various verse forms, dedicated to love, in *Primeros frutos*. They are lyric, free from rhetoric, and often reflect a youthful sentimentality.

The poet's artistic sensitivity to shadings of color is revealed in the poem "Madurez" ("Maturity"), where we find charming variations of gold in his painting of the Asturian landscape. We shall make no attempt to translate it as a poetic entity, but shall merely paraphrase a few examples of his use of nuances of color, and his concluding thought. The poem probably reflects an influence of the French Symbolists. The author of *Primeros frutos* had translated some of this poetry to Spanish before leaving Oviedo, and his translations were published in the local paper, later attracting attention in Madrid, according to Ayala's statement in the interview with Julio Trenas.

"The great mountains, mysterious, distant, . . . are the color of amber, . . . golden / like the cider of the villagers." There flows from "the fountain of gold in the sunset," an incandescent stream of light.

> *(Los grandes montes, misteriosos, lejanos,*
>
> .   .   .   .
>
> *están como de ámbar, son aurinos*
> *como la sidra de los aldeanos.*
> *De la fontana de oro que mana en el poniente,*
> *toma un caudal su curso líquido, incandescente, . . .) (OC.* II, 20)

In "the glow / of the twilight, all is vaguely yellow." / There is "a chromatic scale," ranging / "from the prodigy of flames that crown the sky, / to the diaphanous, soft, straw-colored / reverberation / . . . of the sheaves of reed-grass, / and the burnished fringe / of the waters of the river, the color of orange, / and the dreamy mirror / of the pool, with its reddish veil."

> *(Bajo el brillo*
> *del crepúsculo, es todo vagamente amarillo.*
>
> .   .   .   .
>
> *Una escala cromática sobre lo rubio entona,*
> *desde el prodigio en llamas que los cielos corona,*
> *hasta el diáfano, suave reverberar pajizo*
> *que en la ribera ponen los haces de carrizo,*
> *y la bruñida franja*
> *de las aguas del río, de color de naranja,*
> *y el soñador espejo*
> *del remanso, velado por un color bermejo,)*

"The woods, the dense woods, . . . are copper-colored; / and the gentle mountains, girded in a golden yellow skirt / of soft vegetation. / Everything is golden," the color of his beloved's hair. In the poet's spirit "echoes that sonorous song / which the Universe plays on its golden lyre."

> *(y los bosques, los densos bosques, que están cobrizos;*
> *y las dulces montañas, ceñidas en su falda*
> *de sutiles vegetaciones gualda.*
> *Todo es rubio, ¡ay Amor!, del color de tus rizos.*
> *En mi espíritu hace eco ese canto sonoro*
> *que el Universo tañe en su lira de oro). (OC.* II, 21)

Despite the warm beauty of this golden harmony, the poet becomes melancholy, recalling his unfortunate longing for knowledge, seeking "the great truths of men / in the austere confines of learned libraries." He found nothing but "hollow words. / Good and Evil, Death and Life, God." All that he had learned "are words, words, words without meaning."

> (*Escudriñé las grandes verdades de los hombres*
> *en ámbitos adustos de doctas bibliotecas.*
> *Nihil, nihil.* . . . .
> . . . . *palabras huecas.*
> *Bien y Mal, Muerte y Vida, Dios. Cuanto hube aprendido*
> *son palabras, palabras, palabras sin sentido).*

The final stanza is typical of Ayala's change of mood. As he returns to Mother Earth, "carried along in the course / of the ever-changing," he notes parenthetically that "the unchanging dominates, / as after winter comes the spring, / and with the spring the swallow."

> (*Vuelvo hacia ti arrastrado en la carrera*
> *de lo mudable (mas lo inmutable domina),*
> *como tras del invierno vuelve la primavera,*
> *y con la primavera vuelve la golondrina.) (OC, II, 22)*

The theme of Death is found in a poem, "Los umbrales del huerto" ("The Threshold of the Garden"), inspired by the death of a young friend, who has now crossed the threshold of the garden "of the supreme truth, of the Great Beyond" (*de la verdad suprema, del más allá*). The poet is questioning: "Death, the shadow of life? Life, the shadow of death (*¿Muerte, sombra de vida? ¿Vida, sombra de muerte?*).

And again: "What were we? What shall we be? What are we?" And so / I do not know if I am thinking, and if I exist, and if I dream. / But I dream, although not alive, because love is my master. / Love, the only truth and powerful and strong."

> (*¿Qué fuimos? ¿Qué seremos? ¿Qué somos? De esta suerte*
> *si estoy pensando ignoro, y si existo, y si sueño.*
> *Mas sueño, aunque no vivo, porque amor es mi dueño.*
> *Amor, la verdad única y poderoso y fuerte.)*

He addresses his friend: "You have gained the summit of immeasurable love, / of inexhaustible love, of love unfailing." *(Tú has ganado la cumbre del amor sin medida, / del amor sin desmayo, del amor sin flaqueza).* The poet, still uncertain, concludes by thinking of himself, in contrast: "I, meanwhile, here, captive in the live coals of a great love, / do not know whether I live and dream or dream and do not live." *(Yo, en tanto, aquí, en las brásas de un gran amor cautivo, / no sé si vivo y sueño o si sueño y no vivo").* (*OC*, II, 23) His uncertainties recall those of Segismundo, in Calderón's *Life is a Dream,* but unlike Segismundo, he finds no solution. This poem reflects the melancholy of a youthful poet.

Recalling Asturias with nostalgia, Ayala writes of a *Romería,* a religious "Pilgrimage." The golden light of a festival sun covers the path with laughter and the wooded fields with sighs. From the distance comes the golden sound of bells, and the youths in the street are playing flageolets and timbrels. But this happy day, with its charm of color, light, and sound, was long ago. His greatest treasures then were childhood laughter in hours of peace, and above all, the kisses of his mother. He longs for the April hours and the laughter of his childhood. (*OC,* II, 39-40)

Pérez de Ayala was always fond of mixing literary genres, and in this collection of poetry, we find included a "Poema en prosa," a prose poem patterned after Solomon's Song of Songs, omitting, however, the parts of the Bride and the Chorus. The twentieth-century poet, speaking as the Bridegroom, admires the beauty of his beloved, using figures of speech of the modern age and of his own Asturias, at times quite unlike those in the biblical Canticle which reflect the life of Israel, both rural and regal. For example, the Bridegroom likens the hair of his Bride to "a flock of goats streaming down the mountains," but it is also "like draperies of purple; a king is held captive in its tresses." The poet from Asturias finds the hair of his beloved to be like the autumn apples, which have lent it their redness. The sun has given it the gold of noonday, and to her cheeks the rose of dawn. The cheek of the Bride of the Canticle is "like a half pomegranate behind her veil." We find a more delicate simile in likening her breasts to "twin fauns, the young of a gazelle that browse among the lilies." The breasts of the modern maiden are like "twin lambs," and also "white and warm . . . like the wing of a dove."

Although we do not find a description of the maiden's hands in the Canticle, Ayala likens the hand of his beloved to a rustic lily and to a rose: "Five petals has the lily of your hand, with the color and aroma of white lilies; and your fingernails are curved and diaphanous, like the petals of a rosebud." Although written in prose form, the original has the lyric beauty and rhythm of poetry: *Cinco pétalos tiene el lirio aldeano, nacido en las praderas o en las montañas, a la sombra de los álamos; . . . Cinco pétalos tiene el lirio de tu mano, con color y aroma de azucenas, y tus uñas son curvas y diáfanas, como hojas de capullo de rosa.* (P. 47)

Both maidens are pure. The Bridegroom of the Canticle declares to his Bride: "You are beautiful, my beloved, and there is no blemish in you." The maiden of the "Poema en prosa" is *fruta intacta* ("untouched fruit"), and her flesh is surrounded by the "aureole of the archangels." While the Canticle is one of the great lyric masterpieces of the Bible, rich in sensory beauty and parabolic significance, the prose poem by Ayala, though more simple and brief and less ornate, has also great charm, sensory appeal, and lyric beauty.

The limits of this study do not allow us to give more space to the poems of *Primeros frutos,* and it is difficult to make any general evaluation of them. Ayala was enjoying metrical experimentations, as were most of the great poets of the time. His poems are written in a wide variety of verse forms, few of them traditional, though usually with consonantal rhyme and a true lyric quality. There does not seem to be a unifying theme unless it be love, one of the eternal themes of Poetry, according to Ayala's declaration. The other two themes, God and Death, do not have much expression here, which is understandable, for such things seem very far off to youth. Ayala once wrote that "all great poets begin by loving women and Nature very much, and they conclude loving God very much." (*País,* p. 24)

The poems in this collection reveal the varied interests and enthusiasms of the young Pérez de Ayala: his love for his native Asturias and its great natural beauties; his interest in French poetry, not only that of the Symbolists, but also much earlier French poets; his broad knowledge of other world literatures and his humanistic training, with frequent and spontaneous references to mythical and legendary figures of the Greek and

Latin world; his longing to know the mysteries of life and death;
and many nostalgic memories of his youth and his early loves.
In them we find the youthful voice of a true lyric poet.

III   La paz del sendero (The Peaceful Path)

In 1903, Pérez de Ayala published the first volume of his
proposed tetralogy on man's path through life, *La paz del sendero
(The Peaceful Path)*. It is the poem of adolescence, the poem
of his native soil. Shortly before its publication, he wrote a
letter to a friend, the first part in poetry and the closing part in
prose, in which he announced the coming publication of this
volume of poetry and described it as "neither very pretty nor
very ugly, done in the manner of Berceo, nature lover and
dreamer, . . . a sane and logical book, . . . very human, a bit
mystical, somewhat pastoral, and somewhat ecological." (*OC*, II,
20)

The first poem, which gives title to the volume, is written in
the *mester de clerecía*, consisting of a fourteen-syllable verse in a
four-line mono-rhyme stanza, used by the thirteenth-century
Benedictine, Gonzalo de Berceo, and others of the *mester*, the
"cleric's school of versification." Pérez de Ayala was obviously
inspired in this opening selection by Berceo's poem which serves
as Introduction to his volume, *Milagros de Nuestra Señora
(Miracles of Our Lady)*. However, the *Milagros* has forty-seven
stanzas, filled with considerable allegory, while the poem of
Ayala has only seven stanzas and lacks the allegory. Both poets
present themselves as weary pilgrims on the path of life. The
poets' ages were quite different at the time of writing. Berceo
was probably at least in middle age, while Ayala was about
twenty-two years old. Both poets, weary of their wanderings,
found great peace in the beauties of nature. The youthful poet
presents himself thus:

> With sackcloth of bitterness, a pilgrim of life,
> after long wandering I came upon the peace of a path.
> The last splendor of the day was dying.
> On the summit of a poplar sobbed a linnet.
> (*Con sayal de amarguras, de la vida romero,*
> *topé tras luenga andanza con la paz de un sendero.*
> *Fenecía del día el resplandor postrero.*
> *En la cima de un álamo sollozaba un jilguero.*) (*OC*, II, 83)

The poet continues: "In no place on earth was there the peace that reigned there. / It seemed that God dwelt in the countryside." *(No hubo en lugar de tierra la paz que allí reinaba. / Parecía que Dios en el campo moraba).* He notes the celestial perfume of the honeysuckle and the white buds of wild roses, the peaks of the poplars against the sky, the sound of cattle bells blending with the song of the linnet, and his heart is filled with emotion.

The charms of nature are specifically named by Ayala, while the description by the more primitive Berceo is more generic, thus following medieval tradition. However, Berceo does name specific fruit trees such as the fig and the apple.

The young poet is arrested by the greeting of a youth, hailing him as a stranger. The poet assures him that he is no stranger. In this land he was born, and here he wishes to die. And he concludes: "In the peace of the path my soul was submerged, / which from emotion dared not weep. / The night was falling." *(En la paz del sendero se anegó el alma mía, / que de emoción no osó llorar. / Atardecía).* (*OC*, II, 84) The poem closes with nightfall, a bucolic tradition since the days of Virgil. These opening verses of the volume dedicated to youth reflect the poet's love of his native soil and a nostalgic appreciation of its beauties on his return.

Other poems of the volume continue in the same mood. In "Almas paralíticas" ("Paralytic Souls"), he revisits the country home of his youth, after a year's absence, and the house assumes life for him and seems to look upon him with the solicitous love of a grandmother. Her look consoles him in his grief, as he recalls his mother who had been with him there a year ago. It is evident that she had died in the interval, for he now calls himself an orphan. The house and the peace of nature mitigate his sorrow. Even the vine arbor salutes him affably and sobs with love and gratitude at the poet's greeting.

He reflects with melancholy that, on visiting an old house that has been closed, "one hears the swift course of human existence, / which runs toward death without ever stopping." *(se escucha el raudo curso de la humana existencia, / que corre hacia la muerte sin detenerse nunca).* For him: "The house is a rock which the river of life / has left behind in its rapid current." *(La casa es una roca que el río de la vida / ha dejado atrás en su rápida corriente).* (*OC*, II, 86) He finds empty cups and half-open

books in the library, which evoke old sorrows. His country home
is a little old lady who envelops him in her maternal charm and
whispers counsels.

The poet loves old churches and convents and humble houses,
each with its particular voice and aroma which reveal its soul.
He decries the person who seeks meaning in surface reality.
Everything is in repose under the golden stars and the mysterious
blue light of the moon, and his solitude finds comfort in the peace
of the countryside, as he hears the distant voice of a countryman,
singing a melancholy song to his beloved.

In the poem "Dos valetudinarios" ("Two Valetudinarians"),
the two are an old armchair and a mahogany dressing table,
which evoke memories of his childhood and his mother, who
sat in the armchair, fatally ill, but smiling gently in her suffering.
Various critics have pointed out that some of these verses are
a direct imitation of a poem by the nineteenth-century nature-
loving French poet, Francis Jammes. Salvador de Madariaga,
in his *Genius of Spain*, compares one of Jammes' French stanzas
with a similar stanza by Ayala. Both selections are somewhat
simple and sentimental.

Ayala has no hesitation in admitting the direct inspiration of
Francis Jammes, and remarks also that he has translated here and
there a line from other foreign poets. He intended to print
these lines in italics, but for a later edition it was impossible
for him to recall their source, and he had lost the original version
which had the references. (*OC*, II, 134) In an interview with
Andrés González Blanco, he remarked that he had been accused
of stealing from Francis Jammes, and he concluded ironically
that perhaps he might not write more verses because he did not
find them sufficiently beautiful in any author to appropriate them.
(*OC*, I, xxxvii)

While there is only one poem in this volume by Ayala that
has a marked similarity to a poem of Jammes, in the latter's
volume of poetry, *De l'Angelus de l'aube à l'Angelus du soir*
(1906), there is similarity to Ayala in themes, such as nature,
love of the land and its creatures, and in the style, intimate,
sentimental, and melancholy.

In Ayala's poem, "Nuestra señora de los poetas" ("Our Lady of
the Poets"), Our Lady is the moon. There is again a note of
weary melancholy at the beginning, as the poet writes: "There

is twilight in my soul / and there is twilight in the sky." *(Hay crepúsculo en mi alma / y hay crepúsculo en el cielo)*. The monotonous grey darkens and envelops his heart. The moon appears and he declares his love for her, but she coquettishly hides behind a cloud, later to reappear, and his heart is filled with love in the landscape. The poet closes the long poem with "Salmos" ("Psalms"), verses strongly reminiscent of the "Noche Serena" ("Serene Night") of Fray Luis de León:

> When I see the sheepfold of silver fleece
> in the empyreal heavens pasturing on constellations,
> I think that a Holy Shepherd tends it for me,
> only for me, who dream in the village night.

> *(Cuando veo el aprisco de plateados vellones*
> *en los cielos empíreos pacer constelaciones,*
> *pienso que un Pastor Santo por mí lo pastorea,*
> *sólo por mí, que sueño en la noche de aldea.)* (*OC*, II, 107)

"So my poor soul sought night and day / springs of joy and fountains of happiness." *(Así mi pobre alma buscaba noche y día / manantiales de gozo y fuentes de alegría)*. He crossed mountains and valleys, but all was a chimera, and men turned aside at his misfortune. The poet addresses himself once more to the Holy Shepherd:

> Only you, Holy Shepherd, attentive to my lament,
> over the night extend your countless flocks,
> and because my soul is clad in a tunic of illusions,
> you offer it the white shelter of their fleece.

> *(Sólo tú, Pastor Santo, a mi lamento atento,*
> *sobre la noche extiendes tus rebaños sin cuento,*
> *y porque el alma vista túnica de ilusiones,*
> *le ofreces el abrigo blanco de sus toisones.)* (*OC*, II, 108)

And finally the divine moon, "whiter than snow, softer than the breeze / that moon which is at once a tear and a smile" *(más blanca que la nieve, más suave que la brisa / esa luna que a un tiempo es lágrima y sonrisa,)* has penetrated his innermost being.

The theme of love is delicately treated in two poems, "El poema de tu voz" ("The poem of your Voice"), and "Tu mano me dice adiós" ("Your Hand Bids me Farewell"). Both poems express a somewhat exaggerated youthful melancholy and sentimentality. In the former, the poet was so moved by a feminine voice, "like a spring in the / desert / of my existence" *(como un manantial en el / desierto de mi existencia)*, (*OC*, II, 111) that he wept. The latter is a lyric exaltation of his native soil which he is leaving, as the hand of his beloved bids him farewell.

The theme of death is found in the final poem, *"Epílogo"* ("Epilogue"). The gold of autumn has come, and its voice

> is a gentle sigh of Nature
> which infuses men with its majestic calm
> so that in the moment of abandoning life
> we may do it gently, without weeping the departure,
>
> *(es un leve suspiro de la Naturaleza,*
> *que a los hombres infunde su majestuosa calma*
> *para que en el momento de abandonar la vida*
> *lo hagamos dulcemente, sin llorar la partida.)* (*OC*, II, 123)

But the poet's soul has not yet learned to die. He reflects:

> My poor soul has not the knowledge of a rose,
> imprisoned in the vase, severed from the rosebush.
> It is a butterfly
> who loves the springtime and adores life
> because it fears death. . . . .
>
> *(Mi pobre alma no sabe lo que sabe una rosa,*
> *en el florero presa, del rosal desprendida.*
> *Es una mariposa*
> *que ama la primavera y que adora la vida*
> *porque teme la muerte. . . . .*

He adores the countryside that has cured his ills, and concludes:

> In it I would spend the autumn days
> if they were not a monotonous prelude to winter,
> if I did not look at the sky which on diamond fingers
> spins subtle threads of rain on its thousand distaffs,
> the bare trees which shiver constantly,
> and under my footsteps rustle the dead leaves.

(Con él permaneciera los días otoñales,
si no fueran monótonos preludios del invierno,
si no mirara el cielo que en dedos de diamante
hila sutiles hilos de lluvia en sus mil ruecas,
los árboles desnudos que tiritan constante-
mente, y bajo mis pasos crujen las hojas secas.) (OC, II, 124)

There is charming imagery in these final verses and in many poems of this volume which constitutes a "struggle to apprehend the supernal Loveliness," as we may gather from these words by Edgar Allan Poe, quoted as a preliminary to the volume. Pérez de Ayala has found this "Loveliness" in the countryside of his youth, Asturias, and in the peace of Nature. He has given it his own kind of poetic life. His approach to reality is personal and subjective, youthful, sentimental, melancholy, full of sensory appeal. The poet has said that "the imagination is nourished only by the senses." *(OC, II, 562)* His emotions are intimate, sincere, and delicate, and naturally less mature than in his later poems. He is capable of handling both the archaic verse form of Gonzalo de Berceo and the varied verse forms of the modern poets, in his own original way.

Rubén Darío, in a eulogistic prologue to the first edition of *La paz del sendero,* wrote that "from these springtime years comes the voice of a profound and thoughtful poet. . . . It is a sentimental springtime, the color of autumn." He finds Ayala intensely modern, possessed of great ingenuity, interested in renovation of form, and one of the new poets who think. *(OC, II, 71-73)* This judgment by Rubén Darío is understanding, well-expressed, and prophetic. Some of the best poems of twentieth-century Spanish poetry are to be found in Pérez de Ayala's later volumes.

IV El sendero innumerable (The Path of Infinite Variations)

Although Pérez de Ayala continued to write poetry, his next volume of poems, *El sendero innumerable (The Path of Infinite Variations),* was not published until 1916. In the interval from 1903 to 1916, he lived a very full and active life, publishing four major novels, doing considerable journalistic work, and experiencing the benefits of much travel. He lived in England, Italy,

and Germany, and spent some time in France. He visited the
United States, where he married his charming American wife.
During this visit, he sent back numerous articles to Madrid
newspapers before his return to Spain in December, 1913. His
first son, Juan, was born in Madrid in late 1914.

In this second volume of poetry, besides the first poem (1905),
and the final one (1915), very few of the poems are dated, but
almost all reflect a greater maturity and a more universal outlook.
As we have noted, the poems of Ayala's first volume are personal,
intimate, sentimental reflections, recollections, and impressions
of the poet's native land. In the volume dedicated to the sea,
the reality is not only the beauty of the sea itself as perceived
by the senses, but especially the sea itself as a symbol, in its
endless movements and variations, of life everchanging. The sea
offers innumerable paths from which man may choose. Atuned
to the subject matter, there is a variety of versification, with
much more movement than in the earlier poems, and the tone
is more intellectual and philosophical.

The first poem, "La Playa," presents "The Beach" with its
changing moments, its gulls, and its tides. There is a charming
description of the incoming wave:

> Look at the wave. It comes over the convulsive blue,
> crowned with lilies, clothed with sonorous
> crystal, and throws itself down with a majestic impulse,
> and sings, and dies, and is submerged in the golden sand.

> (*Mira la ola. Viene sobre el azul convulso,*
> *coronada de lirios, vestida de sonoro*
> *cristal, y se derrumba con majestuoso impulso,*
> *y canta, y muere, y se sume en la arena de oro.*)

There follows the poet's exhortation to man to imitate the tide:

> Go, man, in the eternal flux of things.
> Move toward death with majestic step,
> Clothe yourself with purity, crown yourself with roses,
> and sing as you fuse into the golden sunset.

> (*Vete, hombre, así en el flujo eterno de las cosas.*
> *Resbala hacia la muerte con majestuoso paso,*
> *vístete de pureza, corónate de rosas,*
> *y canta al derretirte sobre el aurino ocaso.*) (*OC*, II, 211)

In "El barco viejo," the poet glimpsing "The Old Boat" in an estuary, recalls his father, who loved the sea. This poem, with the subtitle, "In Memoriam," returns to the intimate mood of many of the poems of *La paz del sendero*, reflecting the poet's childhood by the sea and family scenes with his mother and father, who had recently died. His father left him not a material but a spiritual heritage:

> An honorable soul, a sincere heart,
> ambition for what is noble,
> pity for the plebeian.

> (*alma honrada, corazón sincero,*
> *ambición de lo noble,*
> *piedad por lo plebeyo.) (OC*, II, 219)

The poet hopes that it may be said of him, as it was said of his father: "He is a man." The poem is narrative and sentimental, but appealing in its expression of filial devotion.

As a vantage point from which to view the sea, the poet has chosen a high and impressive rock: "It is a Cyclopean cranium. It is a mind / formidable and granitic." (*Es un cráneo ciclópeo. Es una mente / formidable y granítica). (OC*, II, 227) Here he comes every day to contemplate the infinite paths of the sea, which resolve themselves into two: the path of Venus and the path of Christ; "The path of profane love, the path of sacred love," (*Senda de amor profano. Senda de sacro amor). (OC*, II, 229) On each of these paths the pilgrim will find seven stations, one group representing the seven Christian virtues, and the other the corresponding capital sins. At each of the stations, a chorus sings of the respective vices and virtues.

The poet, confused by the terrible enigma, closes his eyes to meditate, when he hears the voice of an emaciated man, singing of "la primera novia," his first sweetheart. Though their love was mutual, and they vowed it to be everlasting, he left, and on his return he found her married to another, and he concludes: "But the Past / is now irreparable. The Future is uncertain. / and the Present does not exist." (*Mas el Pasado / es ya lo irreparable. El Futuro es incierto. / Y el Presente no existe). (OC*, II, 243)

There follows a delightfully ironic dialogue between Doña Gaviota and Don Cuervo (Mistress Seagull and Mr. Crow), reminiscent in tone of some of the scenes in Juan Ruiz's *Libro de buen amor (Book of Good Love)*. Mistress Seagull thinks that this emaciated man is an idiot to bemoan so vociferously his lost love and to think that the world is a curse. Mr. Crow feels that the man's lament is full of meaning, reminding us of the brevity of life and its illusions. Mistress Seagull is going to fly off to catch a fish, and he is shocked at her cannibalism. He eats dead meat, which to her is indecent. He assures her that she cannot understand, for she lacks tradition. She is not like the aristocratic swan. For Mistress Seagull, the swan is no more worthy of admiration than the goose. The irony and the contrast are typical of Pérez de Ayala.

In "La última novia" ("The Last Sweetheart"), the sea is lashed by a hurricane, but facing it on a rock is a human figure, the "robust man." The main part of this poem is the "Song of the Robust Man," obviously inspired in content and in its free-verse form by Walt Whitman's "Song of Myself," the opening lines of which are quoted as a prelude to the poem, as well as some lines from Gabriel d'Annunzio. The poem by Whitman is much longer than that of Ayala. The robust man in each case sings of his supreme strength and plenitude, and at the same time of his brother. He feels the universe within his robust body and his strong soul, and he knows that the spirit of God is the Father of his spirit. He fears not death, *la última novia,* for it is sent by the Father. His senses are made of the substance of the universe and the essence of eternity. Feeling an everlasting harmony with the universe in body and soul, he wants to be fused with the sea. He plunges in, but despite his strength he is drowned. There is a smile on his lips. Again, the ironic ending is typical of Ayala.

The gull and the crow still soar above, and their dialogue is in ironic contrast to the substance of the poem. This time it is the crow who calls the man an idiot for having given his beautiful body to the fishes instead of dying on land like any good Christian. The gull does not care to discuss it and flies off to sea.

An important poem in this volume is "Polémica entre la tierra y el mar" ("Polemic between the Land and the Sea"). The land recriminates the sea for its inconstancy, for its attempt to vie with the great mountains of the land, for the mountains of the sea are but foam that collapse in an instant. The land comments:

In my calm you will see
that God has his dwelling.
In you lives Satan
who is eternal movement.

(En mi sosiego verás
que Dios hace su aposento.
En ti vive Satanás,
que es eterno movimiento.)
(OC, II, 257)

The sea addresses the land as a "poor paralytic matron," and asks her:

What would not you give to change position
and to break into active pieces,
and to dance in eternal madness,
with a thousand million arms and legs,
like my countless waves
—silver, emerald, sapphire—,
which are born, dance a moment,
sing and cease to exist? . . .

(¿Qué no darías por cambiar de postura,
y por romperte en activos pedazos,
y por danzar, en eterna locura,
con mil millones de piernas y brazos,
como son mis ondas sin cuento
—argento, esmeralda, zafir—,
que nacen, danzan un momento;
cantan y dejan de existir? . . .*) (OC*, II, 258)

It is interesting to note the variation in meter here. The land, which is order and peace, speaks in quatrains and roundelays, while the sea expresses its lively movements and variations in more lively and varied meters. The land is delighted with its inalterable structure and repose. The sea loves liberty and anarchy.

The poem ends ironically, as both land and sea waver in their convictions. The sea admits that it is weary of its movement and desirous of rest. If it were only possible for the two to exchange for just a moment! She would be the land, and the land would be the sea. And the land agrees: "Oh Sea! Oh Sea! / If for only a moment! . . ." (*¡Oh Mar! ¡Oh Mar! / ¡Siquiera por un solo instante! . . .*) (*OC,* II, 261).

A charming "Ejemplo" or "Exemplary Lesson" concerns St. Augustine strolling on the beach, striving to grasp the mystery

of the Holy Trinity. He comes upon a little boy trying to put
the sea into a little hole in the sand. The prelate declares it a
useless undertaking, but the child replies:

> Great is the sea and pitiful the hole.
> But greater is the mystery one and ternary,
> and less sufficient the mind of man.
> Much greater! Much less!
>
> *(Grande es el mar y es el hoyo mezquino.*
> *Pero es más grande el misterio uno y trino,*
> *y es más angosta del hombre la mente.*
> *¡Mucho mayor! ¡Mucho menor!) (OC, II, 263)*

St. Augustine remained absorbed, but when he saw the child
fly away, he knew that he had been admonished by an angel
of the Lord. He knelt in penance for his sin of the intellect, his
thirst for knowledge, and his sin of pride in wanting to know
what only God knows.

Pérez de Ayala creates a beautiful pictorial effect in color and
line, in his painting of the scene:

> And everything was so beautiful,
> so very beautiful and pure
> —the polished sand of gold,
> the sea in spirals curled,
> the blue sky, with a black bird
> and a white bird,
> and the bishop, pontifical,
> with cape in silver and gold embroidered,
> and in the background mountains of violet
> with crests the color of nard . . .
>
> *(Y todo era tan bello,*
> *tan pulquérrimo y cándido*
> *—el pulido arenal de oro,*
> *el mar en volutas rizado,*
> *el cielo añil, con un pájaro negro*
> *y un pájaro blanco,*
> *y el obispo, de pontifical,*
> *con capa de tisú briscado,*
> *y al fondo unos montes violeta*
> *con las crestas color de nardo . . .) (OC, II, 263)*

All is beautiful, pure and static, almost unreal.

Finally, the poet abandons the sea with its innumerable variations, to return to his native soil. He feels the salt of the sea on his tongue and in his soul as "the incorruptible salt of baptism." He is filled with a blind faith and a harmony between his spirit and, the world of things. While returning, he sees on the path a youth, the figure of himself twelve years ago, when he went forth to contemplate the innumerable paths of the sea. He wishes the youth well, that he may discover the great truth and fear not the final truth. And may he have a happy return. May he find peace as the poet has found it, after his communion with the world, in which he has finally found harmony.

Salvador de Madariaga feels that at times in the poetry of Pérez de Ayala there is "too much thought or too little emotion," which "may prevent the soaring of poetry." There should be a nice balance between the two. However, his final evaluation of *El sendero innumerable* is very favorable: "Nothing so satisfactorily complete, so deeply philosophical, and so truly poetical as the pages in which Ayala has interpreted the many souls and the one soul of the sea—a symbol of the many souls and the one soul of man and the world—nothing so earnest and so beautiful, so ample, so minutely exact, has probably been written in modern Spanish verse."[1] We agree with him that the best poetry of Pérez de Ayala is found in this and the third volume of the series.

V   El sendero andante (The Flowing Path)

The volume, *El sendero andante (The Flowing Path),* devoted to the river, which links the land and the sea, was published in 1921, some time after the other two books of poems. However, it contains quite a few selections bearing dates which indicate that they were written previous to the volume to the sea and seeming to anticipate it.

In the interval, 1916 to 1921, Pérez de Ayala was engaged in many and varied activities. In the year of the appearance of *El sendero innumerable* (1916), he published his three short poematic novels: *Prometeo (Prometheus); Luz de domingo (Sunday Sunlight);* and *La caída de los Limones (The Fall of the House of Limón).* He also wrote various articles on the tragedy of the First World War. He was sent to the Italian Front as correspondent for *La Prensa* of Buenos Aires and wrote articles for them, later published in the volume *Hermann, encadenado*

(Herman, in Chains), 1917. He became interested in theatrical criticism, this interest manifesting itself in his two volumes of *Las máscaras (The Masks),* 1917, 1919.

He was active in politics, critical of the government. He was a great devotee of bullfighting, as evidenced in his volume, *Política y toros (Politics and Bulls),* 1918. In the company of his wife, Ayala made his second trip to the United States (1919-1920), during which he sent to *El Sol* in Madrid and to *La Prensa* in Buenos Aires a number of articles on diverse subjects, social, political, and cultural.

While the dates of the poems of *El sendero andante,* as already noted, cover a considerable span of time, the tone in general is modern, mature, often universal. Valbuena Prat considers this volume "the best of the poetry of Ayala, above all in its sense of modernity." He considers the opening poem on the river (1920) to be at the same time "an undulation of images and a summation of ideas of the author and his epoch." He finds the "metaphors personal and deep in beauty."[2] Ayala's description of the river is very lyrical:

> How the river flows and runs and sings!
> And it thinks that it is moving at will . . .
> Now it is like a lance, firm and straight . . .
> Now it bends like a blade of steel.

> *(¡Cóme fluye y corre y canta el río!*
> *y él piensa que se mueve a su arbitrio . . .*
> *Ahora es como una lanza, firme y derecho . . .*
> *Ahora se dobla como hoja de acero.) (OC,* II, 141)

Valbuena finds in the following lines the "fatal pessimism" of the Generation of 1898:

> It thinks that it is doing what it wants.
> And what does it do? It obeys.
> It obeys, unwittingly, the caprices of the land,
> and the law of the earth and sky,
> which send it to sink its treasure
> in the broad abyss of death: the sea.

> *(Piensa que hace lo que quiere.*
> *¿Y qué hace? Obedece.*

> *Obedece, sin sospecharlo, a los caprichos del terreno,*
> *y a la ley de la tierra y del cielo,*
> *que le envían a hundir su caudal*
> *en la ancha sima de la muerte: el mar.) (OC, II, 142)*

We find neither fatalism nor pessimism necessarily in these lines. The concept of the river's flowing into the sea, which is death, is a tradition which has been expressed for many centuries. A notable example is found in the famous *Coplas* of Jorge Manrique. Whether the thought inspires pessimism depends on the individual's temperament and belief. And again according to temperament and belief, one may find fatalism in obedience to the law of earth and sky, or it may be conformity to God's law which rules heaven and earth. Whatever one may believe, he will find a lyric beauty in these lines and this whole poem by Ayala which captures every moment and mood of the river.

Space does not allow us to comment on many of the poems of this volume. We should like to give attention to one relatively long poem on "La prensa" ("The Press"), a seemingly mundane subject, which Ayala poeticizes in a modern and original manner. The poem consists of various parts. In the first, the poet addresses himself to the sleeping newspaper reader, unaware of the world. Awakening, he reaches for the newspaper and becomes master of space and time. From his "Microcosmos," he emerges into the "Macrocosmos." As he holds the newspaper in his hand, he may be unaware of the tenacious effort of generations to produce this modern miracle.

The voice of the rotary printing press is heard, filled with feverish enthusiasm, declaring herself "an infinite matrix," creating countless reproductions of the written word. "In the beginning was the Word," and this was oral and transitory. But now history is woven on the turning wheels of the press.

There follows the "Romance de los periodistas oscuros" ("The Ballad of the Obscure Journalists") who toil at night so that the morning reader may become master of the land. They have sworn themselves to be knights errant and are arbiters of letters, arts, and politics. They are like Alonso Quijano, the Good, who watched while Sancho slept. Their obscure lives will be rewarded at death only by the tears of the Housekeeper and the Niece.

Ayala devotes a ballad also to the Cathedral and the Newspaper with an impressive description of the Cathedral:

countless pinnacles, trembling,
rising pyramids of flame,
which on the passing of a great breath of mystery
were to remain petrified;
fragile buttresses, suspended
in the air by the power of grace;
the tower solid and transparent,
grave and slight, firm and carved,
which a legion of granite devils,
together with a multitude of animals
and lustful flowers of sin,
climb from the base to the cross,
struggling in vain to capture
the cross, like children on a greased pole,
while at the fruitless competition
the gargoyles laugh with their monstrous mouths, . . .

(pináculos sin cuento; temblorosas,
eréctiles pirámides de llama,
que al paso de un gran soplo de misterio
hubieron de quedar petrificadas;
los botareles frágiles, suspensos
en el aire por obra de la gracia;
la torre mazorral y transparente
grave y leve, maciza y cincelada,
que una legión de diablos de granito,
junto con muchedumbre de alimañas
y lujuriosas flores de pecado,
desde el cimiento hasta la cruz escalan,
luchando en vano por apoderarse
de la cruz, como niños en cucaña,
en tanto de la estéril competencia
con su boca monstruosa ríen las gárgolas, . . . (OC, II, 188-89)

The poet describes the portals with their statues of the blessed,
the glorious stained-glass windows, and all of the interior with its
altars of gold and marble and other beauties. Many anonymous
lives have been spent in achieving all this beauty.

Likewise, every line and every news column is nothing less than
an artistic piece created by an unknown hand. The poet reviews
the transmission of ideas from the oral word, the stone tablets of
Moses, the parchments buried in monastic libraries, to the printing
press, whose invention he ascribes, not to Gutenberg, but to

Laurens Coster of Holland, an opinion confirmed by H. G. Wells, in his *Outline of History.*

Even the linotype has its poetry, its potential for good or evil. The type

> are now grains of wheat
> or grains of dynamite;
> they are the mad atoms
> which Lucretius saw
> forming the Cosmos and engendering
> good or evil, tears of a smile,
> according to whether they blend happily
> or with disharmony.

> *(son, ya granos de trigo*
> *o ya granos de dinamita;*
> *son los átomos locos*
> *que Lucrecio veía*
> *formando el Cosmos y engendrando*
> *el bien o el mal, el llanto o la sonrisa,*
> *según se casan felizmente*
> *o con desharmonía.* (OC, II, 195)

Composer, linotypists, editors, and the director, all have their power for good or evil. They may offer the horn of plenty, filled with fruits and gifts, or the cursed box of Pandora, full of rancor and grief. "All depends on the judgment / of a sovereign will." *(Todo depende de un arbitrio / de una voluntad soberana)* The question remains: "Whether the press remade the world or destroyed it . . . , / the morrow will give the arduous judgment." *(Si la prensa rehizo el mundo o lo deshizo . . . , / la ardua sentencia la dará el mañana.)* (OC, II, 196).

Ayala has not only described with poetic beauty the cathedral, reminiscent of similar descriptions by Azorín, but he has given poetic quality to such a modern thing as the printing press. Each is the anonymous record of its time.

We find a charming philosophical note in the poem "Doctrinal de vida y naturaleza" ("A Lesson from Life and Nature"). The poet went happily forth in the springtime, crossing a meadow of velvet green. Suddenly he was filled with consternation to find that his footsteps had crushed the beautiful blades of grass.

He knew not how to flee without causing further destruction,
but, as he watched, the blades of grass, by the virtue of Nature,
rose again, and his footsteps were erased.

> And the breeze sang to him:
> Make your soul smooth and soft,
> like a meadow of fine grass.
> There will pass over it sorrows,
> there will pass over it chimeras,
> there will pass over it virtues,
> there will pass over it griefs, . . .

> *(Haz tu alma lisa y mullida,*
> *como prado de fina hierba.*
> *Pasarán sobre él dolores,*
> *Pasarán sobre él quimeras,*
> *pasarán sobre él las virtudes,*
> *pasarán sobre él las tristezas, . . .) (OC, II, 198)*

Both evil and good will come, wild beasts and white doves. But
none of this will matter, for the soul will be reborn under all
the aspects of Nature, the sun, the breeze, the rain, the night,
and the seasons, until the Reaper comes to gather the old harvest,
to give time and space to the new. The poet exhorts the soul to
remember.

> that you are like the hay in the meadows,
> green at dawn and withered at eve.
> And on withering, your essence
> will fly free, at last free.
> And may it ascend to God!

> *(que eres como heno en las eras,*
> *verde a la aurora y por la tarde mustio.*
> *Y al mustiarte, tu esencia*
> *volará libre, por fin libre.*
> *¡Y que hasta Dios ascienda!) (OC, II, 199)*

One of the most impressive poems of this volume is "El niño
en la playa" ("The Child on the Beach"). Here again, Ayala
reveals his love of contrast in his portrayal of the power of the
waves and the delicacy of the child. With great lyricism and
strong movement and rhythm he describes the waves:

Over the beach, barren and patient
come the waves in a clamor;
they come running with insolent fury,
crushing each other insistently.

.   .   .   .

In their own fury they are consumed,
and on the bare sand they sink.

(Sobre la playa yerma y paciente
llegan las olas en algarabía;
llegan corriendo con furia insolente,
atropellándose a porfía.

.   .   .   .

En su propio furor se consumen,
y en la arena yerma se sumen.) (OC, II, 200)

They come from unknown regions, far off in space and time,
and they are centuries old.

They are like dragons,
they are like horrid monsters,
their jaws open and wary,
jaws mobile and absorbent
with which they swallow the ship and the mariners.
And the snowy foam is their snowy teeth.

(Son como dragones,
son como vestiglos;
las fauces abiertas y cautas,
fauces móviles y absorbentes
con que tragan la nao y los nautas.
Y la nevada espuma son los nevados dientes.) (OC, II, 200-201)

Their deafening roar and impetuous exertion are astonishing
and terrifying, but each wave finally dies like a snowy lamb
delivered to sacrifice.

In contrast with the terror of the waves, we see the delicate
figure of the child:

A flower that assumes the grace of the world;
a flower where laughs the joy of the world;
a flower born of worldly love;
the most delicate flower of the world;

flower of the universe, which bears a name
pure as ermine,
like tomorrow or yesterday, profound.
CHILD:
heaven, earth, angel and man.

(Flor que asumes la gracia del mundo;
flor donde ríe la alegría del mundo;
flor nacida del amor del mundo;
flor la más delicada del mundo;
flor del universo, que llevas un nombre
puro como el armiño,
como el mañana o el ayer, profundo.
NIÑO:
cielo, tierra, ángel y hombre.) (OC, II, 201)

The child, playing on the beach, is imitating the surging and
ebbing of the tide. Suddenly he is terrified by the roar of an
approaching wave. "Oh, if the dragon with its jaws overtakes the
child!" *(¡Ay, si el dragón con sus fauces alcanza la florecilla!)*
The child flees in terror, but the wave, dying down, "licks the
feet of the child, with a cold and hypocritical tongue." *(le lame
los pies al niño, con lengua hipócrita y fría.) (OC, II, 202)*

The poem closes with the "Doctrina," the "lesson." When the
child becomes a man, he will be besieged, not by these fierce
waves but by the dragons of passion, vanity, and envy, but he
must not let them overtake him, remembering that monsters
lose their primitive ferocity. They may lick his feet with a cold
and hypocritical tongue, or they may become like lambs to be
offered as victims to the Goddess Pity.

The poem "Castilla" is interesting in subject matter which
reflects the spirit of the members of the Generation of 1898 with
their preoccupation for the tragedies of the humble people and
the evils of Spain, but with an irony typical of Ayala. The poem is
especially reminiscent of some of the essays of Azorín in his
volume, *España*. "Castilla" contains two parts. The first, "Los
buhoneros" ("The Itinerant Workers"), portrays a family of five
with two burros, all emaciated, crossing the plains of Castile in
their humble cart. The baby girl is very ill, and they seek help
from the villagers, who reject them vigorously, insisting that
they have brought the plague. The doctor's pronouncement is

that the child has died of hunger, and she is prepared for burial with all the trinkets which these poor *buhoneros* possess. The church bells ring as they continue their desolate journey across the Castilian plain.

The second Castilian sketch, "La Cenicienta" ("Cinderella"), portrays the four Giles sisters, all ugly, wealthy, and with suitors, for there is property for all but their poor orphaned cousin, Clementina, whom they have taken in as a servant. All that the four sisters lack in charm and beauty, she possesses. But she has no suitors, for, as Ayala cynically remarks, in "noble Castile," if a girl is poor, she is a spinster. Clementina toils from dawn to nightfall, but her cousins call her lazy. She sings as she toils. Her life is now a dream, for she once read of the love of Lancelot and Guinevere, and she knows that her knight will come riding on a white horse, will kiss her, abduct her, and marry her.

She sings with a pitiful voice a repeated line: "For that man I would give my whole life" *(Por ese hombre daría mi vida entera)*. But the man does not arrive in this village, lying silent in the heat. "The street is vacant. The doors are closed" *(Está vacía la calle. Están cerradas las puertas.)* (*OC*, II, 205) The poem opens and closes with the same note, the somnolent indifference of the village, and the reader is moved to pity for the futile efforts of these humble people.

The volume closes with the poem "Filosofía" ("Philosophy"), regarded by various critics as expressing Ayala's basic belief in the "essential oneness of life." Salvador de Madariaga points out in *The Genius of Spain:* "Ayala is Spanish, . . . he belongs to a race whose natural bent is to consider man as the centre of things. His way, therefore, of poetically understanding nature consists rather in discovering in nature the human—not man's ephemeral moods and feelings, but the permanently and universally human which is Man. This obviously leads to the identification of man and nature as two different forms of one and the same life. All is one and the same." (Pp. 80-81)

The stanzas are varied but with a charming lyric quality and an effective assonant rhyme with the vowels "i" and "o." Ayala portrays man and nature, the seasons, types, sounds. For example:

> Flight of birds—predictions—;
> sails on the marine horizon;

rolling of the waters of the river;
the sound of bells—burial or baptism—;
smoke, cloud, shadow, vague echo.
All is one and the same.

(Vuelo de las aves—auspicios—;
velas en el horizonte marino;
rodar de las aguas del río;
son de campanas—entierro o bautizo—;
humo, nube, sombra, eco indistinto.
Todo es uno y lo mismo.) (OC, II, 206)

This last line is repeated at the end of most of the stanzas.
And all is both fleeting and divine:

All is fleeting,	*(Todo es fugitivo,*
all is ephemeral,	*todo es efímero,*
before the Infinite.	*ante el Infinito.*
But at the same time,	*Pero, al tiempo mismo,*
all is divine . . .	*todo es divino . . . (OC, 206-7)*

The poet concludes his "Filosofía" thus: "Totality? An impossible dream. Harmony. Aim at this goal. / The just and the
harmonious, one and the same!" (*¿Totalidad? Sueño imposible.*
Harmonía. Apuntad a ese hito. / ¡Lo justo y lo harmonioso, uno
y lo mismo!) (OC, II, 208).

Madariaga finds that in this poem, "the idea is developed with
the skill, finesse, and rhythmical elegance which our poet so
easily reaches under his intellectual inspiration." (P. 81)

VI El sendero ardiente (The Fiery Path)

Pérez de Ayala, as already noted, had planned to write two
more volumes of poetry on man's pathway through life, related
to the later periods of his life and to other elements of the cosmos:
El sendero ardiente (The Fiery Path), a poem of maturity and
of man's purification by fire; and *El sendero de cristal (The Path*
of Crystal), the poem of man's liberation and contemplation, corresponding to his old age. This, as the poet said, should be clear
and crystal like the air and the sky. The final poem was never
written, as far as anyone knows.

According to his biographer, J. García Mercadal, Pérez de

Ayala wrote some of the poems of *El sendero ardiente* during a brief interlude in Biarritz, in 1938. In his interview with Riopérez y Milá, in 1959, Ayala referred to working again on these poems, which he was anxious to finish soon.

In the interval between his third volume and this last one, the poet had lived a full and varied life. He had published a number of successful novels and several volumes of essays. He had intervened to some extent in Spanish politics. He had spent five years in London as Spanish Ambassador to Great Britain. He had seen the beginning of the Spanish Civil War and spent several years thereafter in France.

In 1949, he went to South America by invitation to give lectures in various countries, and then resided in Buenos Aires until 1954 when he returned to Spain, due to the death of his elder son. This was a crushing blow which left him with little desire for creative writing. Not all that transpired during these years was conducive to the completion of his original poetic project.

The collection of poems of *El sendero ardiente* was not published until the appearance of Volume II of Ayala's *Obras Completas* in 1965, after the writer's death. According to J. García Mercadal, *El sendero ardiente* was left unfinished, and the dates of the poems composing the collection seem to be unknown. It contains some thirty sonnets in addition to the opening poem, "El sendero de fuego" ("The Path of Fire"), written in *terza rima*, obviously inspired by Dante, somewhat more as to form than as to content. Thus we see that Ayala has abandoned the varied metrics of the Modernists and returned to traditional forms. While Dante came upon the dark wood in the middle of the journey of life, our Spanish poet came upon it in descent, and the dark forest suddenly burst into flames.

Instead of the wild beasts encountered by Dante, here the poet is beset by flames that throw themselves upon him, and a strange voice tells him to abandon all hope, recalling the inscription over Dante's Gate of Hell. The poet will not abandon hope, even in death, as he declares:

> The enclosure of fire is not a wall.
> He who by divine favor passes through it,
> will rise from it more stainless and pure . . .

(El vallador de fuego no es un muro.
Quien por favor divino lo traspasa,
surge de allá más acendrado y puro . . .)

However, he concludes with what seems to be a typically
Ayalan contraindication to his earlier declaration that he will not
abandon hope:

The old life is already falling into ashes.
I long for nothing, as I hope for nothing.
Only pain draws from me a suffering moan.
And thus I pursue the fiery path.

(Cae en cenizas ya la vida vieja.
No añoro nada, como nada espero.
Sólo el dolor me exprime herida queja.
Y así prosigo el ígneo sendero.) (OC, II, 276)

The poet here is not, like Dante, aided by the kindly counsels
of a wise Virgil. While the political as well as the spiritual implications are very important in Dante, in these poems of Ayala
the political aspect is absent. The poet explained in the previously
mentioned interview with Julio Trenas, in 1958, that he was
inspired to write this poetry, seeking an explanation from inert
matter to love, by the poetic work of Lucretius, *De rerum natura*
(Regarding the Nature of Things).[3]

The first poems are largely a polemic between two aspects of
his soul, the spiritual and the sensual, each of which desires to
dominate. In an intellectual and philosophical dialogue, he questions his origin and destiny, seeking a perspective, uncertain
whether he is actor, spectator, culprit, or witness. He only knows
that he exists, but he knows not the why nor wherefore of his
existence. In less personal manner, he observes that man struggles
passively or forcefully to follow the Epicurean philosophy, "to
be himself and to enjoy his life" *(por ser él mismo y disfrutar su*
vida). (OC, II, 279)

If man follows the two instincts declared by Aristotle as
primordial, self-conservation and self-perpetuation, his life differs
little from that of an animal. "The essence of life is hope"
(Esencia del vivir es la esperanza). But the poet asks: "What is
the living soul hoping for? *(¿Qué es lo que está esperando el ser*

viviente?) He can only be hoping for "that which lies beyond the horizon / which continues the present into the future" (. . . *el más allá del horizonte / que prosiga en futuro el presente.*) (*OC*, II, 280).

In the poem "El símbolo de la serpiente" ("The Symbol of the Serpent"), Ayala writes of the primordial humus which nourishes nature and hence man, but eventually man is returned to this humus: "This is the circuit of life. / The serpent biting its own tail." (*Este es el gran circuito de la vida. / La serpiente mordiéndose la cola*") (*OC*, II, 282) This symbol of the serpent was common among ancient philosophies and religions, as for example the Gnostics, and similar to the Chinese "Yang and Yin," as explained by Cirlot, who stresses the essential ambivalence of the serpent and its two aspects, "active and passive, affirmative and negative, constructive and destructive," which form the cycle.[4]

In "Morir habemus" ("We Must Die"), the poet points out the external beauty of Nature, but, in contrast, he finds it frightening within, with the strong seeking to destroy the weak. In this blind struggle, only the human soul has the consciousness of death. The poet, here, does not indicate any hope of immortality, but in the next poem he indicates that "the soul seeks and has a presentiment of a hereafter." (*el alma un más allá presiente y pide*) (*OC*, II, 283) Of course, Lucretius believed that the soul died with the body. In general, Ayala seems to move between hope and no hope, although in his personal philosophy he probably believed in immortality. We may recall his statement that poets usually end by loving God.

The poem "Tempo lento" ("Slow time"), recalls Book VI of *De rerum natura*, in which Lucretius describes the violence of the heavens with their clashing thunder and lightning. If the soul seeks to cast aside "the veil of the immortal," according to Ayala:

> In heaven you will see, more than on earth,
> catastrophic clashes, a mortal duel,
> fearful destruction, a fiery flight.
> Eternally atomic is their war.

> (*En el cielo verás, más que en la tierra,*
> *catastróficos choques, mortal duelo,*
> *horrenda destrucción, fulmíneo vuelo.*
> *Eternamente atómica es su guerra.*)

For "the heaven is not static, it is a whirlwind." *(No es estático el cielo, es torbellino.)* If man is impatient on his path through life, he should reflect that "in that dizzy whirling / a thousand billion years are a second." *(son en aquel girar vertiginoso / mil billones de años un segundo.)* *(OC,* II, 284)

We find that in "Alma Venus," largely a translation of the invocation to Venus with which Lucretius opens his *De rerum natura,* Ayala addresses her as "Mother Venus, root of the living being" *(Madre Venus, raíz del ser viviente).* Her power governs land and sea, and he concludes:

> the earth through her carpets the meadows,
> the sea changes its storms into a smile
> and heaven appeased is flooded with light.

> *(la tierra alfombra en flor por ti los prados,*
> *las borrascas el mar muda en sonrisa*
> *y apaciguado el cielo en luz se inunda.)* *(OC,* II, 286)

For Lucretius, through Venus all life is conceived, rises up, and beholds the light of the sun. The sonnet of Ayala is a condensation of the longer and more detailed invocation of Lucretius.

Ayala follows the line of the Latin poet with poems of the aspects of love manifest in nature and man, "for every being that enjoys life / wishes to outlive himself in blind love." *(que todo ser que de la vida goza / sobrevivirse en ciego amor desea.)* *(OC,* II, 287) He considers the expressions of love in the animal world: "The cock crows arrogantly, the bull lows, / the bird trills, the dove coos," *(Canta arrogante el gallo, muge el toro, / trina el pájaro, arrulla la paloma.)* *(OC,* II, 288) He questions what man resembles in this sonorous world, for one cannot be sure whether man sings or weeps.

In the human world, woman in the dawn of love, is the possessor of all beauty. In the animal world, the lion with his elegant mane is the king of creation, and among animals beauty is the prerogative of males. While love among animals is purely physical, based on instinct, man's love is on a somewhat higher plane. He seeks eternal beauty in woman. In the dawn of human love, asks the poet, is there anything "more beautiful, tender, and pure" than two sweethearts clasping hands and swearing eternal love?

"Oh the divine dawn of human love." (*¡Oh alba divina del amor humano!*) With the first kiss, their souls are fused in an essence "which is the soul of the world." (*OC*, II, 291)

In the poem "Símbolo de la paloma" ("Symbol of the Dove"), Pérez de Ayala abandons the theme of love to write of man's ever having dreamed of flying through the heavens, "to find in swift flight some consolation;/ to learn that which on earth is not known." (*Hallar en raudo vuelo algún consuelo; / saber lo que en la tierra no se sabe.*) It is a pathetic longing of the human soul in its earthly prison, but it is a symbol of "its purest spirit / which aspires to heaven drawn like a magnet, / with the symbol of a bird, the dove" (*. . . su espíritu más puro / que aspira al cielo y que el cielo imana, / con símbolo de un ave, la paloma.*) (*OC*, II, 292)

The symbols of the serpent and the dove are an interesting contrast, the former indicating the inevitable cycle of man's life "from dust to dust," and he seems there to be only a part of the physical world. Neither does the dove offer a solution, but it, at least, indicates that man has higher aspirations than to be merely a part of the physical world.

The final two poems of this collection return once more, as in the early "Poema en prosa" of *Primeros frutos*, to the Song of Songs and the love of Solomon and his Sulamita. The final one is more sensual, and the sonnet form here does not seem to lend itself well to an interpretation of the biblical Canticle, which is much more lyrical than this poem by Ayala.

El sendero ardiente is obviously incomplete. The objective announced in the opening poem, purification by fire, is not achieved, since the final poem terminates the collection on a purely erotic and sensual note. In this collection, after various dialogues with his soul, the poet becomes more general in his speculations on the problems of man's existence, his origin, and destiny, expressed in abstract and philosophical terms, with ideas from Lucretius and Epicurus, and with many rhetorical questions that seem to have for the poet no answer, Christian or otherwise. There is much use of contrast and much less lyricism in this collection, even in the poems pertaining to love, than in his other three *Senderos*.

VII   Ultimos frutos (Last Fruits)

Finally, there is a collection of poems grouped under the title
Ultimos frutos (Last Fruits), which seems to close the creative
poetry of Pérez de Ayala, except for the many poems found in
his novels. The metrics in these last poems are varied, and there
are notes of irony and satire in his criticisms of nature, both
animal and human, and of Spain. He writes of the complacence
of the oyster in its shell, of the amorous activities of the felines,
of the Spanish man who heroically conquers virgin worlds, only
to return to his favorite illusory life and indolence.

In the poem "¡Qué mundo este!" ("What a World This is!"),
Ayala feels that death and burial in the earth are man's inevitable
destiny. "He survives only in love: / to love well is what is
important." *(Sobrevive en el amor: / amar bien es lo que importa.)*
(*OC*, II, 303)

Ayala has written a sonnet expressing true appreciation of
Miguel de Cervantes and his ideal qualities, commenting on his
soul which rejects

> rancor and envy. A soul serene,
> through conforming to the delicate enchantment
> of living and understanding. And making of weeping
> pitying irony. And on the stage
> of the base world, seeking the better side
> of the sinner . . . And preferring him to the saint.

> *(al rencor y la envidia. Alma serena,*
> *por conformarse al delicado encanto*
> *de vivir y entender. Y hacer del llanto*
> *ironía piadosa. Y en la escena*
> *del mundo ruín, buscar la parte buena*
> *del pecador . . . Y anteponerle al santo.)* (*OC*, II, 305)

These ideals are those of Pérez de Ayala, who finds "peace and
consolation" in reading Cervantes, "in sharing his life."

We find an original employment of poetry in the use of the
author's letter in verse to his lifelong friend, the Asturian sculptor,
Don Sebastián Miranda. The poem bears the heading "Argentine
Republic, April (autumn) 1947." The poet reports that he is
alive because he is not dead, but that his soul is divided into two
parts. One part looks to the past, his beloved homeland and his

lifelong friends in Spain; the other looks to the future, not his own, but that of his family. He writes with pride and love of his wife, Mabel; his two sons, Juan and Peque; Carmen, the wife of Juan; and his grandchildren. "How endearing they are! And what rascals!" (*¡Qué cariñosos son! ¡Y qué tunantes!*) (*OC*, II, 312) He appreciates his firm friendships in the New World which alleviate his nostalgia for his native soil and old friends.

Another charming poem in this group is entitled "¡Cuándo será . . . !" ("When will it be!"), inspired obviously by the poem of Fray Luis de León, addressed to Felipe Ruiz de la Torre y Mota. Both poems are in the verse form, the *lira,* first introduced into Spanish poetry from the Italian by the great sixteenth-century poet, Garcilaso de la Vega, in his *canción* "A la flor de Gnido" which begins "Si de mi baja lira . . ." ("If from my humble lyre . . .") It is a lyrical five-line strophe, combining seven- and eleven-syllable lines rhyming aBabB. Fray Luis asks in his poem when will it be that, released from earth, he may fly to heaven to contemplate the pure truth of the cosmos.

Pérez de Ayala begins in a similar way. "When will it be that I can / in liberty and love fly to Spain?" (*¡Cuándo será que pueda / en libertad y amor volar a España!*) (*OC*, II, 314) He longs for the Spanish highlands, Spain's mountains, her streams, her people with all their charming eccentricities. The poem closes with the same lines, "When will it be?" that he can fly to Spain, before he is visited by the Reaper.

Other poems published in the collection of Ayala's poetry, in this second volume of his *Obras completas,* are translations of the classics, from Plautus, Catullus, Virgil. The largest number come from Horace, and some from Tibulus and Prudencio. Also Rodenbach, and Henri de Regnier. They reveal the breadth of Ayala's scholarly knowledge, but, since they are not his original poetry, we shall omit comment on them.

VIII *Evaluation*

We feel that the poetry of Pérez de Ayala has not been properly appreciated. Some readers consider him too intellectual and humanistic to be a true poet. But some of the most sympathetic critics, such as Francisco Agustín, César Barja, Rubén Darío, E. Díez-Canedo, Salvador de Madariaga, and Angel Valbuena

Prat, consider that Pérez de Ayala is one of the outstanding Spanish poets of the twentieth century.

Pérez de Ayala wrote in 1917, in his Prologue to a collection of *Castilian Songs* by Enrique de Mesa, that there are two poles in lyric poetry, *pudor* and *entusiasmo*. The second pole is of course "enthusiasm" in English. It is difficult to find an exact English equivalent for *pudor*. It might be translated as "modesty" or "reticence." Probably the latter is more closely akin to Ayala's idea. He defines it as "the individual lyric power, imprisoned and compressed in the most concealed part of the heart. Enthusiasm is the lyric power in expansion, it is lyricism collectively inflated so that it produces a great unanimous echo. The lyric poet can express his own private sentiments and emotions, or indeed general sentiments." The poetry of the first type is to be read in a low voice; "its essence is absolute subjectivity," and although a thousand readers "may share the sentiments of the poet, each one lives them in his own way," rather than with unanimous enthusiasm. On the other hand, lyric poetry of enthusiasm demands a chorus, "because its origin and purpose is unanimity, and, with different shadings, they all feel it in the same way." (*OC*, II, 506)

At the point of "perfect balance between the two lyric poles of reticence and enthusiasm, . . . with an abundance of ideas closely akin to pure philosophy is true Poetry. The one so inspired is no longer a poet, but the Poet." (*OC*, II, 507)

We feel that these two poles are present in the poetry of Pérez de Ayala, and that very often he achieves the balance and harmony between the two which result in true Poetry. His early poetry represents largely the one pole, reticence, and is to be read in a low voice. It seeks no chorus. It represents lyrically the nostalgic sentiments and emotions of the youth returning to his home after his first early disillusionments. He finds peace in nature and in familiar scenes, and at the same time a melancholy longing for he knows not what, and he fears winter and death.

El sendero innumerable represents the pole of enthusiasm and very often a balance between reticence and enthusiasm with a flow of "ideas closely akin to pure philosophy," and therefore is "true Poetry," as Ayala defined it. César Barja finds poetized in this volume "a certain philosophy . . . with a cordial base," with some exceptions. But "the general is harmony, the essential equilibrium among sentiment, imagination, and the intellect."[5] The philosophy is at times balanced by amusing and ironic contrasts, and the volume has many beautiful lyrical and pictorial effects.

The same may be said of *El sendero andante* with its varied and modern meters, and the original portrayal of "La Prensa," giving such an unusual subject a lyric value. The Press and the Cathedral are both the work of many unknown men, and represent the anonymous record of their respective times.

El sendero ardiente is more difficult to evaluate, since it is incomplete. It is more rhetorical and philosophical, and consequently less lyrical. Intellect seems to outbalance sentiment and imagination, and the harmony so highly valued by Pérez de Ayala is not achieved. But balance and harmony are achieved in many of the poems of these volumes which make them true Poetry, particularly in *El sendero innumerable* and *El sendero andante*.

CHAPTER 3

Four Early Novels of Pérez De Ayala

THE novel is the most definitive contribution of Pérez de Ayala to world literature, and his novels have received acclaim from literary critics in Spain and abroad, both early and late. Although his novelistic career covered a relatively short part of his long life—only a little more than twenty years (1907-1928)—his novels have lived and are still being studied seriously and favorably by literary critics. He published his last fiction, *Justicia (Justice)*, in 1928, but, more than thirty years later, in 1960, he received for his creative writing the Juan March Prize, a Spanish prize of considerable monetary value and of great prestige. It is evident that his novels are read beyond the borders of the Spanish-speaking world, for they have been translated to English, French, German, Italian, Portuguese, Swedish, and Japanese.

At the time of the appearance of his earliest poetry, he was also writing fiction, and among his contributions to the Spanish review, *Helios,* (1903-1904) were several short stories. Throughout his career as a writer of fiction, he wrote a number of short stories later published as collections in such volumes as *Bajo el signo de Artemisa (Under the Sign of Artemisa)*, 1924. (*OC*, II, 865-1004) The author has placed these early stories under Artemisa's sign because Artemisa was the tutelary goddess of youth. The collection contains six short stories, the earliest of which bears the date 1902. The author states that the second story was written in the same period, and all of them are youthful tales, the first two written when he was almost a child. (*OC*, II, 865-66) The first relates an alleged episode in the life of Rabelais, "father of French laughter," who "taught humanity to man." (*OC*, II, 877) These words are significant as showing a natural affinity of Ayala for the French writer.

The limitations of this study preclude the possibility of more than a passing reference to Ayala's short stories and only to the most important of his short novels. We shall confine ourselves to a consideration of his longer novels, which in their trajectory show a marked progress from the local and somewhat autobiographical to universal themes.

I Ayala's Ideas on the Novel

Pérez de Ayala expressed some ideas on the novel in an undated essay that was written sometime between 1952 and 1957. He wrote that "doubtless the vocation and aptitude of a novelist manifest themselves from the beginning, but it is not possible to write the great novel, with all its attributes, before maturity. . . . A great novel of youth can only be a subjective novel." He is convinced that "the author of a great novel must be well equipped with years of life, observation, and experience."[1]

Also, in an essay on "The Art of Writing Novels," he declares that "the essential is inspiration," and he understands inspiration as the "innate qualities of an artist." Furthermore: "The good novelist is characterized by the possession of a universal sympathy."[2]

In the earlier-mentioned interview with Riopérez y Milá, in 1959, Ayala commented: "The novel is above all a condensation of life. One must live first, and afterwards write novels." Hence, it is natural that Ayala's later novels are the really great ones, but we are first concerned with his early novels.

His four earliest novels are: *Tinieblas en las cumbres (Darkness on the Heights)*, 1907; *A. M. D. G.*, 1910; *La pata de la raposa (The Fox's Paw)*, 1912; and *Troteras y danzaderas (Mummers and Dancers)*, 1913. All four novels are filled with a great variety of episodes and episodic characters, some of whom play a principal role in one novel, and in others a minor role or none. Unifying these novels is the psychological study of Alberto, repeatedly unstable, as he aspires to artistic or literary fame, or loses the desires for either. We see in these novels the author's sympathy for unfortunate humanity; his interest in art, literature, and the world about him; and his sincere preoccupations for the problems of Spain.

In 1942, Pérez de Ayala wrote an important Prologue to the Argentine edition of *Troteras y danzaderas*,[3] which unfortunately

is not found in his *Obras completas,* but which explains some of
his intentions and purposes in these early novels. He uses many
episodic characters because each one "represents (or pretends
to represent) fundamental attitudes of the individual conscience
before life, . . . and a vital reaction, defensive or offensive."
(Prologue, p. 5) Again, we see Ayala's desire to seek different
perspectives in a search for vital truths or values.

He further explains that his first four novels are intimately
linked, following his original plan "to reflect and analyze the
crisis of the Hispanic conscience since the beginning of this century." (Prologue, p. 7) This crisis of conscience was first manifest
in the works of the Generation of 1898 and continued evident in
later writers, such as Pérez de Ayala and Ortega y Gasset. Although this crisis of conscience began in Spain, following its defeat by the United States in 1898, it was according to Ayala a
"general historic phenomenon in Europe during the first quarter
of the century," in which the "individual conscience," insecure,
"was centering itself on the axis of the national conscience, with a
single magnetic pole, which is the universal unity of culture, the
life of the spirit in its millenary roots," moving "toward its
destiny, no less remote." (Prologue, p. 11)

In the same period in which Ayala drew up the plan for his
early novels, he had also imagined, as part of the cycle, a poetic
work to be entitled *The Forms, the Clouds, and the Norms,* a
work which was never written. However, in this Prologue, he
explains the project, the ideas of which have also a relation to the
novels.

In the period of *The Forms,* when one is a youth, he feels
their attraction, a sense of being identified with them, and he feels
himself as a new world. In the second period, *The Clouds,* the
forms seem to disappear, to be only deceptive clouds, and man's
spirit feels like an orphan in an indifferent world. But finally, in
the third period, *The Norms,* man finds, with the passing of his
"labors and the days. . . , that the forms are only the perceptible
appearance of the eternal norms," and "that in order to possess the
forms we must first be possessed by the norms; that man cannot
include the universe within his norm, but he must be included
and coordinated by the eternal norms within the universe."
(Prologue, p. 17)

For Ayala, the "eternal norms" are the love with which we were engendered and that with which we shall further propagate ourselves; the land in which we were born, and the fatherland to which our native soil belongs. The "vital values" are "religion, ethics, and aesthetics." These norms and values man can neither create nor destroy. He can only "live them, feel them, and understand them, in an obedience and collaboration, equally pleasant and fruitful, and the more he realizes them in his life, the more his passage through life becomes universal." The greater or less originality of the individual man is found, not in his extraordinary position, work or conduct, "but in the degree of intelligent and persuasive penetration with which he perceives . . . the inviolable harmony of the eternal norms and the vital values." (Prologue, p. 17)

The ideas of the proposed poetic work are important, since, according to the author, his novelistic plan was to be a complement to the poetic one. In these four novels it appears that the forms are still deceptive clouds, and man feels like an orphan. Ayala declares that he wrote these four novels in "the useful zone and analytic stage of bitter truths and hard reality." He feels, however, that "there is latent in them a certain proximity . . . although invisible, to the final poetic truth, that of the eternal norms and vital values." (Prologue, p. 18)

II Tinieblas en las cumbres (Darkness on the Heights)

This first novel, *Tinieblas en las cumbres*, (*OC*, I), was written in 1905 but was not published until 1907. The author assigned to the novel a didactic purpose, but it is evident that he had some qualms about its publication. He wrote under the pseudonym Plotino Cuevas.

Prior to the publication of the novel in 1907, Pérez de Ayala wrote to his much-admired friend, Pérez Galdós, requesting that he write to his sole remaining loved one, his father, in defense of the novel, with the purpose of softening the insults and denunciations which he was sure would come with its publication. In his letter, Ayala assured Galdós that the thought in it "is noble, is elevated, it is perhaps profoundly religious."[4] We find no record that Galdós wrote the requested letter, but that he approved of the novel is certain. In preliminary words for a later edition, Galdós praised the novel highly and declared: "It has enchanted me, it has fascinated me. I consider it a masterpiece of picaresque literature. Truth, humor, sentiment, reality, ideality, all are in it. And in wealth of diction, I do not believe that anyone can equal it."[5]

The first edition of the novel had a Prologue signed by Padre X of the Society of Jesus, which in subsequent editions has appeared as an Epilogue. In this appendage to the novel, the alleged author, Plotino Cuevas, is on his deathbed, attended by the priest. After a long confession and final absolution, Plotino Cuevas hands Father X a manuscript and extracts from him a promise that the priest will attend to its publication as a dreadful lesson to youth, "who may see themselves in that mirror, conceive horror, and flee from the path of evil." (*OC*, I, 235)

Besides the Epilogue, the novel has three parts. In the first, "Prolegómonos" ("Preliminary Observation"), the reader is given the description of several dubious young men who are making arrangements for a trip to the mountain heights above Pilares (Oviedo) to see a total eclipse of the sun. The group will consist of five young men accompanied by five young prostitutes. The atmosphere is somewhat in the picaresque tradition, as Galdós says, picturing a world of no moral preoccupations. Ayala points out that the history of prostitution has a very long literary tradition, going back at least to the days of Babylon. The most important young man in the group is Alberto Díaz de Guzmán, weak, but of rather high standards, possessed of artistic aspirations, although he plays only a small role in most of the novel. One of the prostitutes, Rosina, is important, for both she and Alberto appear in several later novels of the tetralogy.

The second part of the novel, "El pasado," is a flashback into the "past" of Rosina and her innocent childhood and youth in a humble family of mariners. In reaction to her father's desire that she marry a successful but gross factory proprietor, she suddenly falls in love with Fernando, the strong man of a passing acrobatic circus, yielding voluntarily to his advances. As a result, she flees from home, bears a child, and becomes a prostitute, apparently unrepelled by her new profession.

The third part, "La jornada," is the story of "The Trip" by train and on foot to the Asturian heights by this carefree and boisterous group, engaged in amorous activities and much eating and drinking. Their language is in tune with their activties and social level. In contrast, there are various descriptions by the author of the countryside and the mountains, which are lyrical and beautiful.

Alberto remains somewhat aloof from the group, interested only in Rosina, the young novice in her profession. On the heights, Alberto encounters a former English acqauintance, Adam Warble, popularly called Yiddy. Here Ayala departs from his narrative technique and continues in a kind of dramatic dialogue between the two, first suggesting to the reader that he skip it since it has nothing vital to do with the story.

However, the dialogue (*OC*, I, 179-98) is important and has a somewhat autobiographical value in the words of Alberto, who explains to Yiddy his great love of nature and beauty, a love so intense that it sometimes causes him to weep. He has decided to be an artist because of his fear of death. He feels that art is the only road to glory and immortality. He had wanted to be a writer but concluded that painting was the only universal art, since it has no language barrier and can be understood as well by a Patagonian as an Aragonese. Although he does not believe in heaven or hell, he does believe in an afterlife, as he says: "I believe in something mysterious, of very subtle essence, which, infused into our body, gives it life and must survive it." But in what form, he does not know. And he continues: "That we are to ascend to a higher existence, for me is undoubtable; but shall we conserve the memory of our earthly and corporeal pilgrimage?" (*OC*, I, 195) Yiddy believes that life never ends, but that it is transformed.

As they talked, the white mist became increasingly dense and sad, giving an eerie atmosphere to the scene with its rugged rocks, its forests of dark pines, greenish oaks and chestnuts, acquiring a yellow efflorescence. Little green valleys "shone like emeralds," and the cliffs "like diamonds." The author's description of this nature is impressive, and Alberto found it "formidable and sublime." He felt how the "livid penumbra, which insidiously and slowly spread over the earth, infiltrated his spirit," and "a tragic chill seemed to run over the surface of the earth." (*OC*, I, 211)

As he watched, "a sea of darkness . . . was spreading violently, deliriously, dizzily over heaven and earth," and "a wave of infinite obscurity was approaching him, enveloping him, swallowing him. He fell to the ground in fear." (*OC*, I, 214)

We see here the symbolism of the novel's title, as Alberto

explains to Yiddy: "I had in my soul crystal and pure heights; the darkness has penetrated within me, it has destroyed and annihilated everything. I shall never see the light." (*OC*, I, 215) He has abandoned hope and concludes: "It is preferable to die, once and for all, than to live constantly waiting for definitive death." (*OC*, I, 217) Following the advice of Yiddy, he rejoins the carousing group who abandon themselves to unrestrained drinking. His philosophy is now to "eat, drink, and be merry."

The true eclipse is in Alberto's soul, as Ayala explains in his aforementioned Prologue to *Troteras y danzaderas:* "Love, beauty, religion, morals, art, literature, whose ideal validity was already uncertain for him, because of the previous morose and corrosive action of a conscience in a critical and dissolving attitude, lose suddenly all their vital meaning; they are nothing but fallacious shadows within the absolute and fatal darkness." (P. 15)

Despite this declaration by Pérez de Ayala, there is a scene toward the end of the novel which might indicate a glimmering, innate hope. Alfredo, in his drunken state, is making his way home with Rosina, when he is suddenly moved to enter a church, and there he prays: "Oh God; My God! God of my childhood, . . . give me light, give me the light of the soul, and the clear light of the spirit!" (*OC*, I, 225) While he is thoroughly intoxicated, we may recall the words, *in vino veritas*. In wine there is truth, which may come to the surface, involuntarily, in the uninhibited state of inebriation.

While Ayala has given more space to Rosina's past and the libidinous trip of these bacchanalians, we feel that the most important part of the book deals with Alberto, with his unstable character, his artistic and spiritual aspirations, and his groping for the values of life, which may also reflect the author's own artistic and spiritual inquietudes, the beginnings of the progress of the artist.

Agustín finds the novel "neither moral nor pornographic, a novel, realistic and human," but he feels that "it is better to show virtues than correct vices." (p. 103) It is possible that the alleged didactic purpose of the novel achieves its goal, for one may, as Ayala puts it, "conceive horror," or at least be repelled by the crude language and bare realism of some of the scenes among these revellers, but these aspects appear frequently in the contemporary novel in world literature. But Ayala does not offer us a tragic vision of life. These people are happy as they are, except for Alberto. Their portrayal recalls the ironic amusement and vitality of the Arcipreste de Hita and his mountain girls.

III A.M.D.G. (To the Greater Glory of God)

After the spiritual crisis of Alberto portrayed in the first novel, Ayala reverts to the childhood of his character, seeking to explain his eccentricities as a result of his education, in the novel *A. M. D. G. (To the Greater Glory of God)*, 1910, a bitter criticism of Jesuit education. The author evidently decided in later life that the criticism was excessive, for, on giving permission for the publication of his *Obras completas*, he did so with the explicit provision that *A. M. D. G.* be omitted. Consequently, it is available only in an early edition of his *Obras completas*, or in single copies, difficult to obtain.[6]

In this novel, supposedly autobiographical, Alberto is called by the diminutive, Bertuco. The novel recounts the boy's experiences in the Jesuit school of the Immaculate Conception in Regium (Gijón). The author had received his earlier education in a Jesuit school in San Zoil and certainly was familiar with Jesuit education, of which he here paints a grim picture. Most of these Fathers conduct themselves in a cruel and unchristian manner, a manner which is in bitterly ironic contrast to their motto, *A. M. D. G.*, "To the greater glory of God." They seem to believe that the end justifies any means.

The Rector, as well as the other Fathers, encourage and reward tale-bearing, and, as a result, the children learn to be very secretive. They restrain their complaints, even when they are well justified. Most of the Fathers are governed by pride and a certain disdain for their students. Father Conejo—which translates as "Rabbit"—is in charge of discipline, and is a master detective in discovering misdeeds, which he promptly reports to the Rector. Father Mur ("Mouse") ably assists him and is a despicable character who administers inordinately cruel physical punishments, giving free reign to his own rage with no thought of the glory of God.

More than a novel, the book is a collection of grotesque caricatures of these strange men and their actions. There are, however, several good priests such as Father Urgoiti, described as a "holy man," who lives somewhat outside reality and is kind to his

students, even those unprepared. Father Atienza is another "holy
·man," who lives almost exclusively in his cell, even holding classes
there. He is frequently a victim of the tyranny of the Rector.
Father Atienza is writing a book on evolution. The third good
priest is Father Sequeros, full of tolerance and kindliness, a bit
of a mystic, and he believes that the best kind of discipline is
achieved through love. The two latter priests are favorites of
students and townspeople, consequently drawing upon themselves the envy of other members of the Order.

We do find in the book explanations of the character of
Bertuco. He has skill in drawing and painting, which are fore-
runners of his later artistic aspirations. The school has a system
of awards called *dignidades* ("honors") for good conduct and
premios ("prizes") for application and achievement. Bertuco has
never won a *dignidad* and has no desire for one, believing that
"good conduct and talent are incompatible." (*A. M. D. G.*, p.
159) He prefers talent, and for the keenness of his intelligence
he wins high awards. On his chest is hung "the cross of
emperador."

We learn something of his inner thoughts in a chapter written
as his diary. He is convinced by Jesuit teaching that God punishes
but never pardons, and that He is to be feared rather than loved,
although the child asks God's pardon for this judgment. On the
other hand, he is devoted to the Virgin and writes a charming
little poem to her, begging her help and explaining that he had
never known a mother's love. His own mother had died in his
early childhood, his father took no interest in him, and he was
cared for by a servant woman, now dead, and by an uncle, Don
Alberto, who still assumes responsibility for the boy. The father's
irresponsibility does not reflect Ayala's own childhood, for we
know from his poetry and letters that there was a close bond
between him and his father.

In his search for beauty, Bertuco finds a lentil, which he plants
in an empty toothpaste jar. He is filled with joy and tenderness
as he watches the miracle of its growth. He also loves to listen
to the song of the crickets in the night.

Bertuco had learned about sex the previous summer through
the information of a young seminarian and an experience with
the gardener's daughter. He is horrified by the knowledge he has
acquired, but with passing time he is vaguely fascinated by

feminine charms. Then he pushes this aside, making an effort to replace such interests with more fervent religious activities. Sex is not a great preoccupation of his in this novel, and we can understand his being largely repelled by the sensuality of the bawdy group of Ayala's first novel.

One day, as Bertuco is imitating the gestures of a tambourine player he had recently observed, he is surprised by Father Mur who, believing the boy to be making fun of him with these gestures, takes fierce vengeance upon him, dragging him by the ears, humiliating him, and finally beating him unmercifully. The boy has convulsions and is placed in the infirmary, in a condition so serious that the Reverend Fathers protect themselves by sending for the boy's uncle, Don Alberto, who arrives with a young doctor, Trelles. Bertuco, after these months with the Jesuits in which he had learned the danger of frankness, will tell his uncle nothing, but Don Alberto takes the child home with him the next day.

They are accompanied by Father Atienza, who has decided to leave the Order because a tribunal has refused publication of his lifelong work on evolution, judging it unworthy of a Jesuit. This detail recalls a similar action by Ayala's own professor, Cejador.

Ayala closes the novel with a question put by Dr. Trelles to Father Atienza: "Do you believe that the Company of Jesus should be suppressed?" The reply is instantaneous: "From its roots!" (*A. M. D. G.*, p. 266)

Immediately after the appearance of the novel, José Ortega y Gasset wrote a commentary for the newspaper, *El Imparcial* (Dec. 1910), praising the novel highly. Ortega was in a position to know about this type of education, having studied in a Jesuit school near Málaga. He remarked that he and Ayala had both been *emperadores*, each in his respective school.

Ortega wrote: "This book transcends literature and is valuable as a very significant document for the problem of Spanish pedagogical reform," and furthermore "it is, in everything important, of a great exactitude." He finds one grave fault in that Ayala did not point out clearly "that the radical vice of the Jesuits, and especially of the Spanish Jesuits, does not consist in Machiavellianism, nor in cupidity, nor in pride, but simply and clearly in ignorance." Although he does not favor suppressing anyone in the Spanish national family, he concludes that it might be desirable to suppress the Jesuits for a merely administrative reason, "the intellectual incapacity of the Reverend Fathers."[7]

This novel by Pérez de Ayala and these words by Ortega y Gasset express the opinions of two of the finest minds in European thought in the twentieth century, and they are a strong condemnation of Jesuit education. Yet these two men certainly acquired a fine basic humanistic education in Jesuit schools. They stress the negative aspects and omit the good from which they benefited. Their judgments were probably and understandably affected by the dreary atmosphere and harsh discipline of the schools.

In a small postscript to *A. M. D. G.*, Ayala has written that his "poor book" was "entering the world with the risky pretension of bettering it a little." (*A. M. D. G.*, p. 267) Thus he has indicated a didactic purpose for this novel, as he did for *Tinieblas en las cumbres*. Agustín classifies Ayala as a "pedagogical novelist" in this story as well as in another novel to be discussed later. In defense of the Jesuits, Agustín remarks that they are constantly trying to make their education more attractive to students. He finds the novel well written but inferior to the other novelistic work of Ayala. (Pp. 229-43)

The novel was well received by journalists and critics at the time of its publication. For some reason which has not been possible to ascertain, it reached the stage of the Teatro Beatriz some years later in Madrid. The staging was done by López de Carrión and Martín Galeano. E. Díez Canedo wrote an account of the production for *El Sol* (Nov. 7, 1931), describing the criticism, denunciation, and somewhat violent consequences. No words could be heard from the stage during the first two acts because of the noisy protests of the crowd. There followed blows, broken chairs, until the arrival of the police, who made some forty-five arrests. The final act was acclaimed by the remaining audience, who called for the appearance of the author at the conclusion. He did not appear, for the very good reason that he was at the time in London, serving as Spain's Ambassador to Great Britain.

Later critics such as Valbuena Prat and Eugenio de Nora find this novel somewhat unconvincing and melodramatic.

IV   La pata de la raposa (The Fox's Paw)

Following the publication of *A. M. D. G.*, in 1910, Pérez de Ayala entered into a period of great activity, both writing and traveling. In the fall of 1911, he went to Florence, Italy, to study art. In that fall, besides his study of art, he pursued the courtship of the charming young American, Miss Mabel Rick, who was there studying music and was later to become his wife. At the same time, he finished the third novel of the tetralogy, *La pata de la raposa* (*The Fox's Paw*), signed in Florence in November of 1911.

This novel is composed of three parts, "Night," "Dawn," and "Afternoon," which reflect various transitions in the soul of Alberto, with a variety of characters, and with scenes in various geographical settings. After the second novel, which served as an interlude to explain the early formation of Alberto, this third novel resumes the story of *Tinieblas en las cumbres*, the morning after the trip to see the eclipse, and the disastrous effects of this on the spirit of Alberto.

He awakens, feeling the severe effects of his inebriation, thoroughly disillusioned with any artistic aspirations. He moves about his room, fiercely destroying his books and works of art. Visiting companions of the previous day inform him that the scandalous trip has been reported in the newspaper, and that Alberto has been accused of the subsequent disappearance of Rosina.

Alberto is not especially disturbed by the accusation, but in his state of artistic disillusionment, he decides to seek seclusion in his country home in Cenciella. During the trip his innate aesthetic sense reawakens as he notes the beauty and soft colors of the countryside and the picturesque types of countrymen, who have for him a quaint and pictorial value.

Having arrived at Cenciella, he finds solace in the rustic setting, concentrating his attentions on his favorite companions, two dogs, Azor and Sultán, a rooster whom he calls Alectryon, a cat named Calígula, and he interviews an ant whom he designates as Mme Comino. Alberto finds that these creatures represent various moral aspects. The dog represents the Christian moral, for he recognizes a superior being, his master.

The mystery of death comes into Alberto's thoughts, and he comments: "Our life, at the moment of birth, is like an empty box, whose walls are of black diamond. The walls are death. Our life is limited by death on all sides. With what are we to fill the box?" (*OC,* I, 266) That seems to be a dominant question for Alberto. What is the meaning of life? The cock finds it in sex. The cat is satisfied with the Hellenic moral, believing itself the center of the universe, and that the best of life is to be found in "eating, sleeping, and dreaming." The ant follows a utilitarian moral, working daily, unaware of the abyss of nonexistence. The author devotes meaningful poems to each of them, who eventually end in their own paradise, but man seems unable to profit by their examples.

Finally, there comes to Alberto the memory of his sweetheart, Josefina, normally called Fina, a quiet, meditative girl of classic beauty, and he leaves Cenciella to see her. Their love is renewed, and they are aided by Aunt Anastasia, an elderly spinster, who is a charmingly portrayed character, one of the best of the novel. In the course of his visit to Fina, there is further reference to the accusations against him regarding Rosina. Feeling certain of his innocence, he is undisturbed by probable legal consequences, and Fina has complete faith in him. For Alberto this love is written with a capital letter, and the soul of Fina is what he wants to possess. Theirs is a pure love. Believing that he has found a true meaning to his life in this love, Alberto promises the father of Fina that he will report to the judge and clear up the accusation against him.

The action changes abruptly, in accordance with the author's love of contrast. After the tender and idyllic scenes with Fina, we find Alberto and his future brother-in-law, Telesforo Hurtado, wandering through the streets of Pilares at night, looking at the women, visiting a crude Music Hall, and finally, at the suggestion of Telesforo, visiting a house of ill fame. Alberto is inspired by one of the occupants with a mixed feeling of repulsion and sympathy, but, after succumbing briefly to her charms, he leaves the place horrified with himself. His illusions are gone. He is no longer worthy of Fina. As he walks down the highway, the sight of the moon fills him with aversion, for he sees "in it and its revolutions around a corrupt world, something of himself." (*OC,* I, 318) In a farewell note to Fina, he declares his complete unworthiness and his unalterable love.

Stopping briefly in Cenciella, he turns over his summer estate and some thousands of pesetas to his servant, Manolo, and sets off in pursuit of "the absurd and fantastic," which he finds for a time as a kind of impresario in a traveling circus. Due to his own artistic talents, ingenuity, and ample funds, he is a success. He has decided to "live humor," having found painting the wrong medium for it. He enjoys satire, when nobly exercised.

Having offended a local priest who turns him over to the law, Alberto passes several days in jail, rejecting favors offered him by a friendly judge. He spends his time befriending the prisoners, whom he classifies in three types: morally deficient, corrupted by society, or victims of passion. Pitying them, he determines to devote himself to social justice, once freed from prison. Freedom is quickly achieved, for Rosina, only recently informed of the accusations against him, presents herself in person, thus proving his innocence. This is the "night" used as the title of this part of the novel, a kind of dark night of the soul.

In the novel's second part, "The Dawn," we find Alberto, for no explained reason, enjoying himself in London with the Mackenzie family, a strange nonconformist group. The parents, married after the birth of their two children, are now wealthy and given over to the enjoyment of the senses and alcohol. There is a casual attraction between Alberto and the daughter, Peg Mackenzie. His stay there is terminated by a telegram announcing a large financial loss for him. Telesforo Hurtado, now brother-in-law of Fina, and a banker, has absconded with the funds. It is a cold "dawn," but Alberto faces it philosophically.

Back in Spain, Alberto is advised by his friends to marry Fina who has been awaiting him, but Alberto is not a person to marry her, when she has money and he has none. Seeking peace, he returns to his country home Cenciella, only to be received by his former servant, Manolo, with complete ingratitude and insolence. Manolo has risen to success and denies that he owes Alberto anything.

Visiting the tombs of his ancestors, he suddenly concludes that he has been a dreamer, but now he must do something. But what? He thinks of the eternity to which he too is destined. Evaluating himself, he concludes that he is worth nothing because his whole being is "rotted with softness, because the solitary delight of

dreaming and thinking as a game has corrupted his very bones,"
and he believes "that life . . . is of no value in itself, only in
its adornments," which he wishes to enjoy. (*OC*, I, 412)

In the course of his walks about the countryside, he encounters Aunt Anastasia and Fina, and once again their love is renewed, Fina forgiving and forgetting his long absence. Using
the homely figure of the fox caught in a trap, who gnaws his
way free, even though he may mutilate one paw in the trap,
Aunt Anastasia explains that one should turn his back on the
past, freeing himself from its burden. Alberto, reflecting on her
words, concludes: "The idea of death is the trap; the spirit is
the fox, or the astuteness with which to evade the snares of fate.
. . . Strong spirits" are able to penetrate with clairvoyance "the
excessive beauty of life . . . and they escape from the trap with
muscles tense for action, and with the moving forces of the soul
increased one hundredfold in impetus, power, and efficiency."
(*OC*, I, 427) This, of course, explains the title of the novel.

Ayala once wrote that Alberto loved life because he feared
death. But he seems to be caught repeatedly in the trap of life
from which only Fina can free him. Her love gives him force
and impetus, from time to time, but never consistently.

In this part of the novel, the love scenes between Alberto and
Fina are charmingly enhanced by the presence of Aunt Anastasia,
who witnesses their kissing each other with "passionate chastity."
The dear old lady has always been taught that a kiss is a sin,
but following the scene, she senses "the melancholy of never
having been loved," concluding that "some souls were born to
kiss." (*OC*, I, 429, 430)

Alberto is now fired with a determination to accomplish something to make himself worthy of Fina. He will free himself of the
dragon of the fear of ridicule, inspired in him by the Jesuits.
He will write with a vocation which he believes should be almost
religious, following a Franciscan Ideal, "not to work for love of
money; to distil sensuality into sensitivity; to be obedient, or in
other words, to be sincere with himself." He writes a poem on
"The Ideal," in which he aspires to live in a simple white house
between woods and sea, enjoying nature, his books, and above
all the love of Fina. With this idealistic hope of his "Dawn,"
he departs for Madrid to achieve his goal.

In the third part, "The Afternoon," we find Alberto in Switzerland, enjoying with his artist's eye the beautiful scenes about him. He has achieved some success in the literary world of Madrid. Hurtado, who had absconded with his money, was apprehended in Cuba, and, as a result, Alberto is once again in possession of a large part of his fortune. There is no good reason for his not returning to Fina.

However, his will has changed its course again. His ideals now move toward "the domestication of passions," toward "unity." His purpose is "to intensify the sensation of life, as supreme pleasure." His moral is to be "severe with himself and tolerant of others." His aesthetic ideal is "democratic," and he wishes to elevate "to the dignity of beauty all natural things, to balance the pleasure of living with the uncertainty of knowing." He feels a "universal sympathy for every created thing." He concludes that a woman could offer him only a "sensual and ephemeral pleasure," and hence he cannot consecrate his life to a woman. (*OC,* I, 445) Once again, he writes to break off with Fina, and this time she is convinced that he will not return.

The Mackenzie family, older and more worn, are also in Switzerland. There is a passing play at love between Meg and Alberto, but disgusted with her coquetry and sensuality, Alberto finally informs her that he loves her only as an older brother, or perhaps with a paternal love. The part concludes wth another abrupt change in the orientation of Alberto. He has forgotten the past three years of his life, and after three days of traveling is once more in the garden of Fina, only to be met by the curses of Aunt Anastasia and the news that Fina is dead.

The novel is a good psychoolgical study of Alberto, who has been considered by some critics to be the perfect example of a character completely lacking in will, the type of protagonist frequently portrayed by the writers of the Generation of 1898. We feel that instead of a lack of will, Alberto suffers from a constantly fluctuating will. He determines to do something and usually does it. Then he changes his mind, and his will takes a new course, as he follows new ideals. Alberto is constantly in search of the true values and meaning of life which repeatedly baffle him. He never achieves the harmony and balance which he seeks, as he passes from one psychological state to another in his spiritual disorientation.

This third novel has more unity in its concentration on Alberto

as the protagonist. It is episodic with considerable gaps in time
and place, but it is well written and the characters effectively
presented in all of their variations, one of the best being Aunt
Anastasia. The artistic perception of the author is evident in
his painting of landscapes and types. The language is well expressed, ranging from the dialect of the peasants to the intellectual and philosophical observations of Alberto, who seems
to serve as the *alter ego* of the author. We find some social
criticism, particularly of the judge, lenient toward those with
the proper social connections, and in Alberto's study of the
prisoners' problems.

V   Troteras y danzaderas (Mummers and Dancers)

After his months in Italy, Pérez de Ayala went to Germany
where among other things, he completed his fourth novel,
Troteras y danzaderas (Mummers and Dancers), signed in
Munich on December 10, 1912, and published the following year.
The title derives from a verse from the Arcipreste de Hita,
quoted at the beginning of the book.

This novel portrays a Bohemian world, and is a type which
has a long tradition in world literature. Among specific Spanish
antecedents are *El libro de buen amor* by the fourteenth-century
Arcipreste de Hita, and some of the *novelas* of the early seven-
teenth-century *Exemplary Novels* of Cervantes. This Bohemian
world of Madrid is peopled by innumerable characters, many
of them women of easy virtue or young writers aspiring to
literary fame. Two important themes running through the novel
are the formation of an artist, and social criticism specifically
dealing with the ills of Spain. This second theme follows the
preoccupations of the Generation of 1898.

Troteras y danzaderas fills in the lapse of time between parts
two and three of the preceding novel. The plot of this fourth
novel is very episodic with countless characters, some of them
taken from real life, such as Monte Valdés who is the likeness of
Valle-Inclán, proud, impetuous, and suffering from lack of money
and food. Others will receive mention below.

Alberto Díaz de Guzmán has come to Madrid as he promised
Fina, but now he has largely forgotten her and does not seem
especially interested in achieving fame, though he does pursue
his writing to a certain extent. Rather than a protagonist of the

novel, he seems to be an observer and commentator on various aspects of art and of the world about him. He soon dissipates his recovered fortune and goes to live with Don Angelón Ríos, a rather optimistic and amiable man, who enjoys a nice family home without his family, who live in the provinces, but he lacks monetary resources.

Rosina, the novice prostitute of *Tinieblas en las cumbres*, reappears and is a prominent character in the novel. She is now the mistress of the elderly Don Sabas Sicilia, a government Minister, who furnishes a home and support for her, her blind father, and her little daughter, Rosa Fernanda, fruit of her first amatory experience. Don Sabas is convinced of Rosina's great singing ability and hopes to help her toward a stage career.

Another prominent feminine character is the prostitute, Verónica, who supports her mother and family by her profession. She is the mistress of Don Angelón, who, however, is unable to contribute much financial help. While in the home of Don Sabas, Verónica becomes interested in Alberto, and the interest is mutual. He reads to her his Spanish translation of *Othello* and is delighted with her instinctive reactions which give him a new comprehension of Great Art, which is "a spontaneous flowering of the human spirit and organism," and which takes form in true tragedy. Verónica's reactions move from lyric to dramatic emotion. Alberto concludes that "the tragic spirit is nothing but a clear comprehension of everything created and a cordial justification of all that exists. For the tragic spirit there is no evil born of free will, there are no crimes, but only misfortunes and disastrous actions." He contrasts this with the low and pharisaic art of the melodrama, which "invents free evil, creates the traitor, weaves conflicts between the good and the bad," resulting in sentimentalism. (*OC*, I, 576-77)

Following the reading of *Othello*, Verónica is moved to dance, and her dancing is so spontaneous and expressive that Alberto determines to make her a great dancer, a goal which he later achieves.

Teófilo Pajares may perhaps be called the protagonist of the novel. He is a somewhat hermetic soul, who has been acclaimed as a Modernist poet, but he suffers from the conviction of his own inadequacy and longs for "light." He also suffers from two obsessions, the need for love and the need for money. Without the latter, he can not have the former. He is dominated by a true love for Rosina, longing to make her his, and his alone. Rosina feels a certain kind of love for him, but her love is a product partly of a maternal feeling for him and partly a pity for his poverty.

Teófilo writes and produces a drama, in fact a melodrama of courtly love, which is a tremendous public success, but he is unmoved by the ovations. Walking through the streets with Teófilo that night, Alberto expresses his opinion of this drama as stupid, of many words, but they are high-sounding and hollow. However, he considers it neither better nor worse than much of the Spanish classical theater. More specifically, Alberto feels that Teófilo has aspired to the infinite, is now convinced of the failure of his aspiration, and feels bitter.

Alberto explains further: "The first is nothing less than the desire to ascend to God and 'rub elbows' with Him; the second, a belated discovery that by pretending too much, we have neglected the necessary, and that without reaching gods we have not even become men. It might be said that all Spanish literature, and even thé Spanish character, are filled with these two sentimental norms." (*OC*, I, 760) Teófilo is in such a nervous state that he confesses that he even hates his mother, who has come to Madrid to witness his triumph. Arriving home, he has a violent nervous seizure, but finally retires.

Meanwhile, Rosina has left the loving attention of Don Sabas. After encountering once again the Herculean Fernando, the father of her child, she has decided that he is her true destiny. But at the same time she dislikes leaving the love and respect of Teófilo, as a perfect complement to the love of Fernando.

As evidence of some of the good aspects of Rosina's character, we find the episode of the innocent young provincial girl, Márgara, who, having read of the theatrical and musical triumphs of Rosina, has resolved to follow in her footsteps by first becoming a prostitute. Rosina is determined to prevent this, and Alberto proposes an object lesson. A group, composed of Rosina, Verónica, Márgara, Alberto, Angelón Ríos, and others, make a tour of the brothels of Madrid, going from best to worst, and the sights that greet them are extremely sordid. Márgara returns to her village the following morning in the company of some nuns, who later report that she is entering their Order, and that her piety is exemplary.

Rosina, Teófilo, Verónica, and Alberto spend a brief but idyllic period in a rustic setting on the northern coast, but this is terminated by the news that Fernando is coming to see Rosina. Also Alberto has finishied a novel and is ready to depart for Madrid. After his return to Madrid, Teófilo develops a rapid type of tuberculosis and is attentively cared for by the kindly Verónica. However, he soon dies after making peace with his mother and receiving the last rites of the church.

As we last see Rosina, she appears to be happy with Fernando, despite his regular appropriation of her earnings in the music halls of Paris. Verónica declines the proposal of an honest marriage to pursue her successful career as a dancer in Madrid. Both women are well-portrayed characters.

Discussion of the evils of Spain occurs repeatedly in the novel, but the discussion seems fruitless. Don Sabas, the Minister, feels that his position is useless. He considers the government to be no more useful to the nation than a necktie to masculine attire. It is merely an adornment. (*OC*, I, 521) Later, he remarks that "the ideal can only be achieved with imagination," which the Spanish people lack. "Spain has been a country of chimeras; it has never known what it wanted." The Spanish politician cares nothing for the public good. He does not go into politics "through vocation, but through ambition." (*OC*, I, 704, 705)

Antón Tejero, the fictional counterpart of Ortega y Gasset, is anxious to have a public meeting with orators, for much needs to be done: "Awaken the conscience of the country; inculcate the feeling of political responsibility; purify the political ethics." (*OC*, I, 598) Alberto finds no necessity for the meeting and feels that Spain needs not a political but an aesthetic education, and a sympathy for the external world. Alberto concludes that "without sensitivity and without imagination, sympathy is lacking; and without passing through sympathy one does not arrive at love; without love there can be no moral comprehension, and without moral comprehension there is no tolerance. Spain is a country of absolutists." (*OC*, I, 599)

There is a gathering in the Ateneo to hear a discourse by Raniero Mazorral, presumably the fictional counterpart of the esssayist, Ramiro de Maeztu. The Ateneo is ironically referred to as "the most radiant center of Spanish intellectuality." People gather there to pass the time, and one character declares that their "holy trinity" is composed of "Bulls, politics, and women."

(*OC*, I, 696) Politicians believe that they attract popular attention through their position. "The bullfighters and prostitutes know that they wear the halo of popularity with more decorum and better grace than the politicians." (*OC*, I, 699)

Mazorral in his discourse declared that "Spain had not yet entered into the community of civilized nations; for civilization was synonymous with culture and scientific objectivity," and "hence if Spain hoped to save itself, it must embody culture and become Europeanized." To achieve this, he counseled "two virtues: goodness and work." (*OC*, I, 699) After commenting on the somewhat platitudinous speech, Alberto looks at the group of men about him, one of whom is holding a cat, and remarks: "Mazorral has forgotten that the tutelary genius of the Ateneo is the cat, and that the philosophy of the cat is worth more than all philosophies. It teaches us to be lazy, voluptuous, and elegant." (*OC*, I, 706)

At the end of the novel, a young follower comments to Alberto on a recent article of Tejero's in which he declared that "concern with politics is a waste of time; that one should not be a progressive and a democrat, but a traditionalist, or, what is the same, a restorationist." Tejero declares himself no longer "an objectivist, but a visionary, a Spanish mystic," and the youth questions what Spain has produced. Alberto answers ironically: "Mummers and dancers, my friend; mummers and dancers." (*OC*, I, 815, 816)

Despite all their discussions on the problems of Spain, no one has arrived at a satisfactory solution. Nor has Alberto arrived at any real solution of his own problems, as we see in the final part of *La pata de la raposa*, which completes his saga, and in which he is still the wandering, pleasure-seeking, unstable character who loses Fina, but who reveals a deep comprehension, usually sympathetic, of the world about him. He has reached some success in the literary circles of Madrid, but this is not stressed.

VI *Conclusion*

Pérez de Ayala wrote in his Prologue to the Losada edition of *Troteras y danzaderas* (1942), that these four novels are the first part of an architectonic whole which he was never able to complete. Therefore, we shall not know what plans he had for the further development of Alberto.

Various critics have considered his story to be a kind of autobiography of the author. Norma Urrutia is of the opinion that Alberto is "in many characteristics the portrayal of Pérez de Ayala himself, idealized: perhaps the Pérez de Ayala that he would like to have been."[8] We do not see that any portrayal has been "idealized." It is possible that the writer of the Introduction to *Selections from Pérez de Ayala*[9] was correct in believing that Alberto might be the man Ayala feared he might become. This critic points out the difference between Alberto's vacillating nature and the "intellectual vigor" and "courage" of Ayala as he faces life. If Ayala had some of the early problems of Alberto, he certainly conquered them and emerged undefeated.

Ayala has commented that these novels have considerable autobiographical value "at least in respect to the genesis of the individual spirit, a kind of monograph of an individual soul or inner annals of the formation of a vision of ideas and sentiments with respect to the world."[10]

Since we hear no more about Alberto, we can only assume that he would finally have developed into the strong and fine character of the author. Alberto already has the humor and irony and is developing the essential universal sympathy and comprehension which characterized Ayala. It could probably be said, as indicated elsewhere by Donald Fabian,[11] that in these four novels Alberto has passed through the first two stages in the development of the artist, as explained in Ayala's Prologue, "The Forms," and "The Clouds," and is entering the third stage. "The Norms," bringing a fuller interpenetration with the universe and its "vital values."

Sex is treated frankly in most of these novels, but objectively, not pornographically. It is part of the Bohemian world portrayed. Ayala shows a sympathy for these ladies of ill fame, who often show some good aspects in their characters. The personages are numerous because of Ayala's desire to offer their varying points of view and perspectives on the problems of life. Not only does he present fully his leading characters, but many of the minor characters are well and delightfully portrayed. Ayala has said that "these four novels, and especially *Troteras y danzaderas*, are the purifying filters of tribulation," on the way "to the serenity of Grace." (Prologue, p. 20)

CHAPTER 4

Transitional Short Novels

AFTER finishing the last novel of his early tetralogy, Pérez de Ayala returned from Germany to Spain. In the spring of 1913, he wrote a short novel, *La araña (The Spider)*, name of a small-town café. As this work is of relatively minor importance, we shall omit discussion of it. At the time, Ayala had more important interests than his creative writing.

In the summer of 1913, he made his first trip to the United States to marry the young North American with whom he had fallen in love in Italy. His wedding to Miss Mabel Rick took place in Allentown, Pennsylvania, on September 1, 1913, and the young couple spent some two months in this country before returning to Spain. Ayala, always an eager and keen observer, studied the North American scene and wrote a number of articles for Spanish newspapers, while on his honeymoon. In December of that year, we find him back in Madrid, as evidenced by published letters from him to his good friend, Pérez Galdós. (*Cartas*, p. 16)

His first son, Juan, was born in late 1914, and he had family preoccupations, due to the delicate health of his wife and the care of the child. His interest in creative writing was also diverted by his concern over political and social unrest in Spain, and by the tragedy of World War I.

It was not until 1916 that he published his novels *Prometeo (Prometheus)*, *Luz de domingo (Sunday Sunlight)*, and *La caída de los Limones (The Fall of the House of Limón)*. These novels, published as a single volume, might be called a trilogy unified by the presentation in all of them of various aspects of the problems of Spain. The author has given to each the subtitle, "Poematic novel of Spanish life," and explains that in them still remain traces of "shadows on the heights." However, he seeks here "the poetry of truth by a procedure more direct and synthetic than analytic." (Prologue, p. 19) He includes in this group also the shorter *novels* of *El ombligo del mundo* (*The Umbilical Center of the World*), 1924. At the beginning of each chapter of the three *novelas poemáticas,* Ayala has written a poem which is a lyrical synthesis of the realistic prose to follow, and he uses the same technique in the various parts of *El ombligo del mundo.*[1]

I Prometeo (Prometheus)

The novel *Prometeo (Prometheus)* is the story of a modern Odysseus, with various episodes paralleling the adventures of Ulysses in the Homeric poem. The protagonist is first presented as he escapes from the wiles of Federica, a modern Calypso, on a raft constructed by himself. He is later shipwrecked and takes refuge in nearby woods, where he is discovered nude, the following morning, by the modern Nausicaa, who finds a sheet for him and takes him home.

In the following chapter, the author goes back in time to tell the reader something of this Odysseus, who is, in reality, Juan Marco de Setiñano, a professor of Greek in the University of Pilares, and an ardent admirer of Homer. He was born in Italy of a mother of noble Italian lineage and a Spanish father, described as "handsome, magnificent for his figure and for his laziness." (*OC,* II, 602) After his wife had died, and he had used up all of her fortune available to him, the father threw himself into the River Arno. In most of the novels of Ayala, there are suicides, probably inspired by his sad memory of his own father's death. The young orphan, Juan, described as handsome, manly, taciturn, and proud, is aided by an uncle, who has reserved for the boy a small amount of his mother's former wealth.

In possession of this money, Juan begins to think of his future, finding all horizons too limited for his ambition. He only knows that he wants to be himself. In a conversation with his uncle, he declares also that he wants wisdom, he wants "to know things in all their facets," and even more "in all their hidden meanings and relationships," obviously reflecting the same desire on the part of the author. His uncle assures him that wisdom can be acquired only through "a direct study of Nature and of man," and needs the slow experience of life. (*OC,* II, 604) Juan wants to be both a man of thought and of action.

The boy is attracted by both books and drink. He methodically
reads the best books, both classical and modern, and assimilates
what he reads. He travels about Italy but finds it like a sculpture
already achieved, its tradition deficient and dead. Juan decides
that the true, live tradition must be a trinity of "eternally renewed
force, grace, and astuteness, understanding by active intelligence."
(*OC*, II, 606)

Recalling his Spanish blood, he decides to seek this trinity in
Spain, which he believes to be "the country of possibilities." In
his travels about Spain, always seeking his concept of the trinity
of the live tradition, he finds that in each part at least one of the
three qualities is lacking, and he becomes disillusioned. Many
of his adventures in Spain are likened to those of Homer's
Odysseus.

His love of books and drink continues, and he has gained considerable experience in life, when he arrives in Pilares at the age
of thirty-five. Convinced that his future lies here, he acquires
the professorship and writes his uncle that he has discovered that
Spain is "the country of impossibilities." (*OC*, II, 609)

Juan feels that he is the perfect man, having inherited force
from his father and grace from his mother. The rest he has
acquired himself. But he is, nevertheless, frustrated, for he has
learned that the man of thought must precede the man of action.
He has renounced the joy of being a man of action, for he feels
that it is now too late to achieve what he seeks. He will therefore
engender a son who will be a semi-divine Prometheus, a savior
of mankind, linking heaven and earth. Juan will seek a wife who
has his own essential qualifications, force, beauty, and intelligence.

It is at this point that he becomes interested in Federica, but
soon wearies of her, as we saw at the beginning of the novel.
The story continues his experience with Perpetua, the new Nausicaa, who discovered him like Odysseus, a new-born man, naked
on the beach. He finally acquires some clothes from the gardener's
son, until he can send for his own, and is presented to Perpetua's
aunt, the Marquesa, who is delighted with his handsomeness and
his intelligent conversation. Learning of his Italian origin, she is
sure that he is an Italian prince, traveling incognito. Perpetua's
brothers are less delighted, and there are amusing conversations
among the group. They vie with one another as to who can con-

sume the most food and drink, and Juan easily surpasses the rest, thus winning the respect of some of the men.

All goes well. Perpetua has the qualifications sought by Juan, they are married, and soon expect a son. Juan is delighted, recalling Prometheus who stole fire from the Immortals to give it to man, and foreseeing a great future for his son. He, the man of thought, has engendered a man of action. But the son is born deformed. His back develops a hump. Mentally, he is precocious, but malicious and taciturn. In school, he suffers from the taunts of the students but learns to defend himself with fury.

As the son grows older, he is stirred by the desire for amorous adventures, first making an attempt on a servant and then on a passing milkmaid. The morning following the second attempt, Prometheus is found a suicide, hanging from a fig tree. The best laid plans of men are defeated by the gods.

The tragic irony of the story is obvious. Various critics have pointed out the similarity between this novel and *Amor y pedagogía* by Unamuno. Certainly, they are somewhat similar in plot and in the ending, the tragedy of planned and frustrated parenthood, as the son in each case hangs himself. Both novels can be called satires on scientific pedagogy. But the atmosphere is not the same in the two novels. Unamuno's novel is cold and psuedo-scientific, and most of his characters are unreal. In Ayala's novel, the characters are alive, and there are a warmth and humor about them that appeal to the reader. There are many classical allusions to the adventures of Odysseus, but they are made in an entertaining way. The abstract discourses of the protagonist are less intellectual and more amusing than those of Alberto in the earlier novels. There is much humor in situation and dialogue until the final tragic end which is handled quickly and concisely. The lyric introductions to the chapters add greatly to the whole, the final one giving a foreshadowing of impending failure.

There is an obvious influence here, in both Unamuno's and Ayala's novels, of Nietzsche's theory of the superman, as has been pointed out by Gonzalo Sobejano in his recent interesting study, *Nietzsche en España (Nietzsche in Spain).*[2] As Sobejano says, Ayala is attracted by "faith in the body, in the beauty of the corporal life and in the generation of a perfect being." But he is aware at the same time of "the contemporary level of man's degeneration." (P. 595)

In our opinion, Ayala's ending of his story is far more tragically ironic and effective than that of Unamuno's novel, who adds at the end his repeated theory of the "mother-son" relationship between husband and wife, thus detracting from the tragedy.

For a further understanding of Pérez de Ayala's comprehension and opinions regarding Nietzsche, the reader will find a very illuminating explanation and discussion of "Nietzsche in a Nut-shell," published in *Más divagaciones literarias (Further Literary Musings)*, 1960,[3] the essays dating from 1921 to 1957. Ayala discusses the writings of Nietzsche from the days of his fascination with the music of Wagner, his later break with the great musician after the creation of *Parsifal*, Nietzsche's conviction that God is dead, and his final insanity.

II   Luz de domingo (Sunday Sunlight)

In this short novel, *Luz de domingo (Sunday Sunlight)* literary allusions are not to the classic Greek, but to masterpieces of Spanish literature. Preceding the whole are two lines from the *Poema del Cid* which suggest possible disaster, the thought that how fortunate it would be if the Cid should appear. This is the story of Cástor Cagigal, a lawyer in Cenciella, and his sweetheart Balbina, a charming and innocent young girl. It is April, and they are looking forward to their wedding the following week.

There is a second word of warning in the poem that opens Chapter Two, for the evil snake, asleep in winter, has been awakened by the warmth. The title, *Luz de domingo*, is here explained by the fact that Cástor believes that the Sunday sun is more beautiful than that of any other day.

But this Sunday he is obliged to attend a meeting of the Town Council, of which he is secretary. The Town Council is dominated by two political bands, the Becerriles ("Bovines"), supposedly the aristocratic group, and the Chorizos ("Sausages"), the democratic group. The Becerriles are sons and nephews of the mayor, who has had a dispute with Balbina's grandfather, Señor Joaco, over some land. Also some of the Becerriles are formerly rejected suitors of Balbina. One of the Chorizos warns Cástor that there may be trouble, that he should go only to the meeting, and after that not leave the house of Balbina. Cástor is not greatly disturbed by the warning.

At the beginning of the third chapter, there is an ironic poem with further foreboding in its picture of some of the nobles who, in the past, robbed and raped the villagers, recalling the violence of the despicable Knight Commander in Lope de Vega's play, *Fuenteovejuna*. For a long time, the nobles have been absolute lords. "See the flower of knighthood—and the nobility of long ago!" (*¡Ved la flor de la hidalguía—y la nobleza de antaño!*) (*OC*, II, 647)

Cástor goes to see Balbina after the stormy meeting, where he has again received veiled warnings, and the two take a stroll into the countryside. Cástor has artistic aspirations and has done some paintings in oil in which he considers light more important than color, especially the Sunday sunlight which incites and animates the spirit more than the sunlight of other days. Again we see the author's interest in art. There is a foreboding note when Cástor is saddened to see this Sunday sun set. He declares that it will never return, that the waters of the river on which it now shines will be other waters another Sunday, and they themselves will be different, too.

His foreboding is well founded, when a group of Becerriles appear, seize Cástor and tie him to a tree, and then, before his horrified eyes, all seven successively proceed to rape the innocent girl, who soon becomes unconscious from the attacks. After their dastardly action, the Becerriles wish Cástor a happy honeymoon and nonchalantly depart. This would indeed have been a propitious moment for the appearance of the Cid. Balbina, recovering consciousness, starts running to throw herself into the river, but is stopped by Cástor's pleas to untie him. Once freed, he takes her gently in his arms, kisses her fervently, and calls her his "chaste lily."

The rest of the story recounts their repeated and fruitless efforts to escape from the story of the infamy and the consequent gossip. The poetry opening Chapter Five again recalls the plays of Lope de Vega in which the townspeople seek justice from the king against the evil local rulers, and are encouraged to take their own vengeance. Here the villagers are uninterested in vengeance.

Balbina is ill after the experience, but the wedding takes place as planned, at the insistence of the ever loyal Cástor. Her grandfather has a desperate desire to avenge Balbina's dishonor, which can never be forgotten while others recall it. Balbina becomes pregnant, and the horrible uncertainty of paternity is finally resolved when Cástor discovers on the child's body a birthmark identical to his own.

In seeking a place where their story is unknown, they finally arrive in Castile where the bright sunlight seems to console them, but here, too, someone knows the story. The grandfather decides to resolve the problem by selling all his property. With the proceeds they will go to another world, the world of America.

The poem opening Chapter Eight describes the departure of the ship. Even the sails tremble eagerly to leave this "kingdom of falsehood" for the "kingdom of truth." But again there is a foreboding as the ship takes to sea "in the direction of Eternity." (OC, II, 670) The day is Sunday with its uplifting sunlight. But on the ship they encounter neighbors from Cenciella, who refer to the evils of the Becerriles and report that under the present dominance of the Chorizos, things are worse. Since there can be no justice in Spain, they are departing for the New World.

Cástor is desperate. Their flight will not destroy the bitter memory nor the gossip. On the tenth day, the ship strikes a rock and sinks. Among the few saved are the grandfather and the child. "Cástor and Balbina let themselves die gently" in a close embrace, and their souls fly "to the country of Supreme Harmony, where there exist neither Becerriles nor Chorizos, and there shines eternally the pure and inherent Sabbath sunlight." (OC, II, 672)

This somewhat romantic ending appears to be the inevitable destiny decreed by fate for this young couple who seem too good for the cruel Spanish world portrayed. While Cástor resents the dishonor, he does nothing about it except to try to shield Balbina from the comments of others. Gone are the days when the Spaniard avenged his wrongs. We may recall again the line quoted by Ayala at the beginning. Now there is no Cid Campeador who might intervene in impending disaster, and who did avenge his own dishonor even though it was much less serious than the tragedy of Balbina.

The story is very well structured with the realistic prose of the brief chapters contrasting with the poetic introductions. There is in each of these a growing sense of foreboding, as the author portrays the lamentable characteristics of the political groups and the mayor of the town. It is finally, also a bleak picture of Castile to which Ayala refers in the poetic introduction to Chapter Eight and writes: "Cursed by God is the people—which allows itself to be made miserable, / which bows its neck to the yoke—and bathes its bread in tears." *(Maldito de Dios el pueblo—que deja amiseriar, / que humilla su cuello al yugo—y moja en llanto su pan). (OC,* II, 670) He considers that man cowardly, who lets himself be badly governed. As already mentioned, these deplorable conditions were a favorite subject of the Generation of 1898, but Ayala's presentation of them in this novel is individualistic and artistic, the work of a mature craftsman.

III   La caída de los Limones (The Fall of the House of Limón)

This somewhat longer novel recounts the prominence, decline, and fall of the Limón family. The opening poem presents two women, once fresh roses, now withered with thorns piercing their hearts. How did all this come about? The opening chapter portrays one of Ayala's favorite subjects, a boarding-house, run by Doña Trina. The boarders are average and rustic people, but recently two older women have appeared in the group. They are completely uncommunicative, and Doña Trina will make no explanations. They are obviously spinsters with a great mystery about them, which the narrator proceeds to investigate.

The poem of the second chapter suggests further mystery as the church bells announce a new birth or toll for someone who has died. Mariquita, daughter of Doña Trina, is expecting a baby. One day, the narrator discovers in the sewing room, where they are making white clothes for the expected baby, some pieces of black cloth. The two strange women, Fernanda and Dominica, with a seamstress, are making mourning clothes, which must be ready by the tenth of the month, at noon. Why precisely at twelve? Mariquita explains that before noon these women will not be in mourning, but that after twelve o'clock they will be in mourning, and that they are the Misses Limón of Guadalfranco.

The next linking poem prognosticates the death of an old man, who feels the futility of his undertakings, the vanity of the world, and wants only to die. The author then leaves the scene of the boarding-house in Madrid to narrate the history of the Limón family.

The father, Enrique Limón, an energetic youth, came long

ago to found a small factory in the town of Guadalfranco, bringing in workers and establishing a town club with its entertaining
attributes of card playing and political discussions. He was first
elected deputy and then became the boss of the town and province. He married the lovely young Fernanda, and their first-born,
a girl, was given her mother's name. There followed a long
succession of some thirteen children, all of whom died, and
then a second daughter, Dominica, and finally a son, Arias.
Following his birth, the mother died, leaving the father and
the three children.

Fernanda, of marriageable age when Arias was born, dis-
dained all suitors. She was haughty and uncommunicative. She
followed her father's activities with fascination and came to
share with him the government of the province of Guadalfranco.
As he grew older, she became the true political boss, relegating
the care of her little brother to Dominica and a servant who had
a little son, Bermudo, a faithful companion of Arias. They occupied the rear of the house, where Arias lived like a young
prince with his attendants, as he dreamed of adventures and
wrote poetry which he read to his followers.

They had a devoted old dog whom Arias grew to hate, believing him to be a kind of warlock, the male counterpart of a
witch. As an example of the instability of Arias, on one occasion, in a fit of rage, he kicked the dog so hard that it literally
flew across the garden. Dominica reprimanded him for his
cruelty, and finally, as the dog looked at him pitifully, his rage
turned to remorse, and the dog seemed to pardon him.

As Don Enrique grows old and Fernanda becomes the true
power of the local government, the people resent her authori-
tarianism, an attitude which she chooses to ignore. The father,
who can leave his children little material property, gives them
some final advice on the importance of power, which Fernanda
knows well how to use. He advises them all to remain united.
He finds Arias dazzled with dreams of artistic glory, which has
no practical use. He must achieve high political power and unite
with Fernanda.

The father regards highly the friendship of an ambitious
young lawyer, Próspero Merlo, and sees in him an ideal pro-
spective husband for Dominica. Arias is jealous, wanting Dominica's devotion, which he has always had, exclusively for

himself. Finally, he relents and approves, but with secret anguish, and the marriage is planned for the autumn.

Arias falls in love with love, which he finally bestows on a maiden he has seen in his wanderings through the streets. He does not know her identity, and the faithful Bermudo is amazed at the violent manifestations of this love, as Arias, in solitude, tears his hair and roars.

Each linking poem has a more ominous note. In one, there is reference to Ophelia and Hamlet, with the warning that the torch of love is "in the hands of a madman." (*OC*, II, 705) In the next one, as a new day dawns, "someone will no longer be able to see it." (*OC*, II, 710)

One evening, Próspero Merlo has to visit a wealthy and avaricious widow, on some business. Since she is wealthy, she commands more than a hundred votes in Merlo's district. The following morning, the widow and her daughter are found stabbed to death. Some objects belonging to Merlo are discovered in the house, and he is promptly jailed. The crime is attributed to political motives, and the voice of the people is "Down with the Limones."

Dominica is crushed, and will see no one but Arias, who expresses his conviction that Merlo is not guilty, and in any case the matter can be handled with a little influence from Madrid. Merlo declares firmly that he is innocent. Don Enrique, old and infirm, begs Arias to go to Madrid to settle the affair. Nothing happens but the passing of time, as Dominica remains ill, and the "timid and lazy Arias" postpones his trip to Madrid. The father meanwhile dies.

Finally, Arias comes to Dominica to tell her that he does not want her to be unhappy. She shall marry Merlo, for he, Arias, will go at once to the judge and declare himself the assassin of the widow and her daughter. Dominica refuses to accept such a sacrifice, but Arias assures her that he is indeed the assassin, aided by Bermudo. After the occurrence, he thought it was a dream, but he has questioned Bermudo, who has confirmed the fact that it was no dream but the truth.

Arias relates the whole story to Dominica, his mad love for the unknown girl whom he had discovered to be the widow's daughter, his inability to express himself, his entering her house with Bermudo, after the departure of Merlo. As he ascended the stairs, he saw his beloved standing at the top and was afraid she would call the neighbors. At his command, Bermudo held her. Carried away by her charms and his passion, Arias embraced and raped her. When her mother appeared, the girl attacked Arias, never saying a word, and he stabbed them both to death.

Arias cannot understand his actions, declaring that he had never wished anyone ill and had noble and generous ambitions. He was lazy because he was convinced that he would never achieve them. He slept well the night of his atrocities, and the next day he had forgotten everything, believing it all a dream. And he bids the stunned Dominica farewell. Merlo is released but does not marry Dominica. In a note he tells her that after what has happened, for him she has ceased to exist.

The final chapter returns to the framework of the story, the Madrid boarding-house. In the opening poem, the church bells are again ringing for birth and death. Mariquita has given birth to a son. News of the execution of Arias Limón and his servant, Bermudo, are in the papers. The mysterious ladies of the first chapter, Fernanda and Dominica, appear at lunch, dressed in mourning, their demeanor in somber contrast to that of the remainder of the group, gaily celebrating the birth of Mariquita's son. There is reference to the execution, which Doña Trina hurriedly tries to quiet, revealing the identity of the two women. Those present are amazed. One republican remarks that the older one is then that woman boss, "the worst of all the Limones." In his opinion, she should also be hanged. And the other sister has been covering things up. He concludes: "In this country there is no justice!" (OC, II, 723)

The story is carefully and concisely constructed, its effectiveness greatly enhanced by the various introductory verses with their growing forebodings, leading to the final tragedy. The framework of the boarding-house, with its well-drawn local characters, relieves the somber atmosphere, and these characters offer a strong contrast to the two mysterious and silent sisters.

The character of Arias is well developed, a boy sheltered and supported by his own little court, the devotion of Dominica and the faithful Bermudo. It is evident, beginning with his violent treatment of the dog, that the boy is abnormal. He, like the former Alberto, has ambitions which he is incapable of achieving, due to lack of will, but, unlike Alberto, he responds violently to his sudden emotional frenzies. He is a frustrated youth because of his own weak character, his emotional instability, and his sheltered life.

IV El ombligo del mundo (The Umbilical Center of the World)

El ombligo del mundo (The Umbilical Center of the World) is not chronologically "transitional," as it was published several years later, but, since Pérez de Ayala has viewed it as part of his *novelas poemáticas,* we shall consider it briefly. It consists of a Prologue and five somewhat shorter *novelas.* At the beginning of the Prologue, the author has a note to "the impatient reader," suggesting that he may skip it, if he likes, just as he would skip the entrance steps to a dwelling where he is going to visit. The Prologue opens with a poem informing man that he is his own prisoner, his flesh and spirit the jail and the jailer. He should not be overwhelmed by his own tragedy, but be "a watchtower over time and space." Norma Urrutia considers this volume "the most representative work of Ayala's total novelistic production." (P. 55) We should not go that far in our estimate, but it is an artistic miniature of Spanish types, which might also be called universal, since they have universal weaknesses as well as attractions.

The collection portrays the beautiful northern valley of the Congosto and the village of Reicastro with the various types who believe themselves and their valley to be the umbilical center of the world. Various social classes are presented ranging from simple rustics to a few last representatives of families of ancient lineage. All have their passions and virtues in the tragicomedy of their local life where they amuse themselves, among other things, by giving one another expressive nicknames, a pastime that has entertained Ayala in most of his novels. For example, the leading parish priest is called "Father Eternal." We shall include the two most interesting stories, the second and the last.

In the second story, "La triste Adriana" ("The sad Adriana"), an aspiring poet appears once more in the person of Federico, who spends his time in a café with an intellectual group called the "Scorpions," not viewed with favor by the local conservative priests, such as "Father Eternal." The mayor, of dubious reputation, courts Federico's wife Adriana, largely by letter, during her husband's absences. Adriana, a dreamer who lives outside reality, gives slight response to the mayor's attentions.

In contrast to this couple are her friends, "Calandria," called the lark because her singing rises to heaven, and her sweetheart, Xuanín, who is gradually acquiring a herd of goats. They are lovers of nature and devoted to each other. Xuanín writes simple, primitive poetry which he recites to the two fascinated girls. He is determined to make a princess of his beloved, by his own industry, and they have already decided to name their first-born Salvador or "Savior."

Adriana becomes frightened by the persistent attentions of the mayor, and Federico is enraged at the discovery of one of the mayor's letters, carelessly dropped by Adriana. Rejoining his friends in the café, he is further enraged to learn that a local paper has accused him of plagiarism in his poetry. One of the friends assures him that in the town there is one authentic poet, Xuanín. Federico considers Xuanín an inarticulate idiot. The friend goes on to define poetry as "perfume" and "music." And "above all poetry is concentrated action, latent and supreme action." (*OC*, II, 795) The poetry of Xuanín has all of these qualities.

Meanwhile, the word comes that Xuanín has stabbed the mayor, seriously but not fatally, because of jealousy in connection with "Calandria." Federico rushes home to report to Adriana that the mayor is dead, and he is going to kill her, too. She makes no objection but wants to know who killed the mayor. Federico has to admit with shame that it was not he but Xuanín. She assures her husband of her faithfulness, and their love and understanding are renewed. Their first-born will also be called Salvador. Again Ayala realistically questions whether their happiness will last. Probably not, due to the individual peculiarities of each.

Appealing and human is the final story, "El profesor auxiliar" ("The Substitute Professor"), with its portrayal of Don Clemente and his six attractive daughters. He is described as having a face which reveals "nobility of character and a limited intelligence." (*OC*, II, 851) The family are forced to live very frugally on his meager salary, and the girls supplement the income with varied handwork such as sewing and lacemaking. He is unexpectedly made a substitute professor of Chemistry at the University of Oviedo; the regular professor, appointed through influence, has given up the position, due to his lack of knowledge of chemistry.

Don Clemente has a difficult time with his new students, who do not respect substitute professors and play rowdy tricks on him, a tradition in Spanish universities and institutes, according to the author. One of the worst offenders finally comes to the house of Don Clemente with a box of cigars and a pistol. If the professor consents to pass him without an examination in chemistry for which he is unprepared, the cigars will be his gift. If not, he intends to shoot Don Clemente. But on seeing the poverty of the house and the beauty of the daughters, he is moved by remorse and presents the cigars unconditionally.

The story ends with the frequent humorous irony of Ayala. Two years later the student is married to one of the lovely daughters. Don Clemente is now professor in a religious secondary school, teaching psychology, law, algebra, French, and drawing, for all of which he is unprepared. The character of Don Clemente is well and sympathetically portrayed, and the minor persons of the story are convincingly human. The criticism of Spanish education is an obvious theme in this *novela,* but similar situations could probably be found in many countries.

V *Evaluation*

It is evident, as Ayala wrote, that there is still, as portrayed in these novels, considerable "darkness on the heights," continuing the same line of criticism found in the writings of the Generation of 1898. But here it is done in careful synthesis, more objectively than in Ayala's early novels, with the lyric poems at the beginning of the chapters offering the essential significance of each *novela,* in the manner of the chorus of the ancient classic theater.

Such key verses are also found in earlier Spanish literature, in the choruses of some of the plays of Lope de Vega and the interpolated verses of Cervantes in some of his *Entremeses* (dramatic interludes). We agree with Madariaga, who finds that in the *novelas* of the trilogy, "Ayala reveals himself as a complete artist of fiction," and calls them "little masterpieces of observation, of original creation and arrangement, of truly poetic feeling and

of smiling humor, despite their inexorable Spanish realism."
(*Genius*, p. 82)

One may say that the message in most of these stories is that
man must not let himself be dominated or overcome by apparent
fate. He must not consider himself the umbilical center of the
world. He needs to establish a harmony and balance between
his ambitions and the reality about him. The lyric and the dramatic are artfully interwoven in these short novels by Pérez de
Ayala, and they mark an impressive advance in his novelistic
technique.

CHAPTER 5

Major Novels

AFTER publishing his trilogy of *novelas poemáticas* in 1916, Pérez de Ayala abandoned the writing of novels for the time being. He was invited by the government of Rome to visit the Italian war front, and, for some time, he wrote daily chronicles for the newspaper, *La Prensa*, of Buenos Aires. These chronicles, which we shall consider later, were published in a single volume the following year. There followed other volumes of essays, also to be consdered later, and some of the poetry already studied.

In 1921, Ayala returned to his novelistic interests, writing within the next five years his major novels, in which he abandons the autobiographical note and turns to universal themes. According to his words in the important Prologue of 1942, his purpose in these novels is "the recreation in the present of some of the eternal norms and vital values," (P. 19) which have already been considered in Chapter Three of this study. These major novels are *Belarmino y Apolonio* (1921),[1] the title being the names of the two protagonists of this novel; a novel consisting of two parts, each with its separate title, *Luna de miel, luna de hiel*[2] *(Honeymoon, Bitter Moon)*, 1923, and its continuation, *Los trabajos de Urbano y Simona*[3] *(The Labors of Urbano and Simona)*, 1923; and finally, *Tigre Juan*[4] *(Tiger Juan)*, 1926, and its continuation, *El curandero de su honra*[5] *(The Healer of His Honor)*, 1926.

I Belarmino y Apolonio (Belarmino and Apolonio)

This novel opens with a prologue on "The Philosopher of Boarding-houses," which is an essay-like discussion by Don Amaranto de Fraile, who has spent some forty-five years of his life in boarding-houses. In the opinion of the narrator to whom

95

he was delivering his discourse, Don Amaranto is a "three-peseta Socrates," possessing "ironic pedantry" and "picturesque erudition." According to Don Amaranto, wisdom was sought in olden days in markets, porticos, or gardens, in the Middle Ages in monasteries. Then came the universities, but the best university of present days is the Spanish boarding-house. To live in them, one must be an innate ascetic, for food is scarce, but it is an encyclopedia of knowledge. Little by little, one enters into the individual dramas of his companions. As he contemplates them philosophically, he feels their drama within him.

His listener, obviously the author, much impressed, recalls that here in this boarding-house he had learned the drama of Arias Limón and his sisters. This suggests to him another drama, "half pathetic, half burlesque," which he will save from oblivion, the story of Belarmino and Apolonio.

In the boarding-house he meets a prebendary priest of some forty years of age, normally called Don Guillén, although his father, Apolonio Caramanzana, being both a shoemaker and dramatist, had also given him various first names of famous dramatists of other times. Don Guillén has come to Madrid to deliver sermons during Holy Week, in the chapel of the Royal Palace. He declares himself a believer in God as this should be inherent in his profession. But, in a conversation with the narrator, who has discovered him in his room eating roast beef during Holy Week, Don Guillén explains his reasons for flaunting Lenten rules, comparing Church and State.

In the State there are artificial crimes, and in the Church there are artificial sins. These are artificial if they do not harm justice in the State or dogma in the Church. Don Guillén believes that the State "is a material community maintained for mutual convenience, and the Church a spiritual community supported by mutual love." Discipline in the State is essential to mutual convenience. In the Church, it is a will to sacrifice which needs stimulation in persons who are lukewarm in their faith. For those of firm faith this stimulus in unnecessary, and therefore Don Guillén has no need to practise abstinence. (Pp. 24-25)

Early in the story, there is a suggestion of what will happen in one of the love episodes interwoven with other events in the novel. On his way to his room from the boarding-house one evening, the narrator stops in a café, and, seeing a young woman called Angustias, la Pinta, who resembles a "virgin of Rafael," he draws from her her story.

She is the daughter of a shoemaker-philosopher, Belarmino Pinta, of Pilares. She and the son of Apolonio, the neighboring shoemaker, were in love and eloped, but he was brought home by his father, who ardently disapproved of their marriage, and the wife of Belarmino refused to let Angustias return home. Consequently, she has become a prostitute. The narrator feels great compassion for her. Later, he sees in the room of Don Guillén a picture of a beautiful girl, also resembling a "virgin of Rafael." He declares that he knows the girl, but Don Guillén assures him that it is impossible, that she is his sister, and she does not exist. The novel is told from time to time by Don Guillén, and at other times by the author-narrator. His chapter on the Rúa Ruera seen from two sides has a double purpose, one to describe the street on which the two shoemakers live, and the other to discourse on painters and novelists. Ayala, speaking through Don Amaranto, declares that "to nothing less does the novelist aspire than to create a brief universe." (P. 28) While the novelist has the power to see things in depth, his very art deprives him of the power to reproduce their depth, because his eyes travel over a broad surface and inevitably cover too much. The painter can center his attention on one thing. To describe well, one needs at least two persons to present a scene from different angles. "The important thing is to communicate, manifest oneself and make oneself understood." (P. 29)

Following the advice to seek a dual perspective, the narrator visits the ancient street of Rúa Ruera with two friends, Juan Lirio, a painter, and Pedro Lario. Lirio finds the steet beautiful. Lario finds it horrible, absurd. Lirio insists that the absurd is beautiful, and that the street has life because it is contradictory. No houses are alike, and each bespeaks the individuality and personality of its owner. Lirio loves life because he fears death; he loves art which gives life to things. To prove some of his points Lirio makes a sketch of the street which Lario has to admit is beautiful, although the street is ugly. But art has transformed ugliness into beauty.

On this street is the shop of Belarmino, shoemaker-philosopher, with his wife Xuantipa, a name presumably chosen by the author because of her shrewish nature, very similar to that of Xantippe, the wife of Socrates. Xuantipa is constantly belaboring her husband for his lack of industry, his small earnings, and large debts, but Belarmino suffers her attacks calmly and philosophically, merely remarking that she is an "inferior woman." There are two almost daily visitors to the shop, one the threatening usurer to whom Belarmino is indebted, the other Colignon, a French confectioner, who is generous and cheery and truly loves Belarmino. One great joy in Belarmino's life is the child Angustias whom he loves as though she were the daughter of his own flesh, although she is really the orphaned daughter of his dead sister. He has cared for Angustias since her birth.

His other great joy is his fascination with words, which seem to him to be still in embryo. He seeks to give them new and fuller meanings with his own arbitrary and unconventional interpretations. He is an assiduous reader of the dictionary, calling it the "cosmos" because it contains everything. He looks only at the words and carefully avoids their given meanings. As a result, his speech is in constant need of explanation to the vulgar mind. He is convinced that he is an apprentice-philosopher, since philosophy is simply the broadening of the meaning of language, and only a chosen few will be able to understand him, his language, and his reasonings. He loves to commune with what he considers his inner talent or *inteleto*. As a consequence, the work of his shop, to which he is indifferent, is neglected. He is worried about this at times, but he concludes that "adversity is the mother of wisdom." (P. 59)

Then comes the new shoemaker's shop of Apolonio on the opposite side of the Rúa Ruera. Apolonio announces himself as a "master artist." The townspeople are convinced of the coming ruin of Belarmino. He casually examines the modern and elaborate exterior of the new shop, and smiles innocently and ironically. Apolonio, watching him from within, is disturbed with a strange sense that perhaps in some way Belarmino may come out the winner in their rivalry.

At this point, Don Guillén takes up the story of his father, Apolonio. His family for several generations had served the Count of Valdelulla in Galicia, the eldest son in each generation remaining to serve, while the younger ones went into the Church. The last born Count was a confirmed bachelor, and his sister, married to the Duke of Somovia, had moved to Pilares.

The old Count was interested in the young Apolonio who
seemed to him a precocious child, composing verses and reading
numerous novels and dramas. But the young Apolonio failed for
two consecutive years in the Institute, reportedly because his
excessive imagination prevented concentration and study. However, he always thereafter referred to himself as having received
an "academic education." He wished to be a dramatist, but, when
told that such a career was impossible, he concluded that if he
could not be a dramatist, he would be a shoemaker.

He first opened a shop in Santiago de Compostela, but when
the old Count died, he left Apolonio a small legacy to be handled
by his sister, the Duchess of Somovia. Hence the move to Pilares,
where she is now administering affairs for his modern shop. The
Duchess delights Apolonio with her big heart, her flamboyant
personality, and her tendency to swear when it occurs to her to
do so. She also smokes cigars and holds *tertulias* with only men
present. Her name is Beatriz like that of Dante's beloved, and
Apolonio falls in love with her in his own way. Apolonio has
strange talents. Everything which he says tends to come forth
in verse. This bores the Duchess, who summarily orders him to
speak in prose or not speak at all.

Apolonio and his son are installed in their new shop, and the
boy becomes a friend of Angustias, the daughter of Belarmino.
Shortly thereafter, Belarmino's shop is closed by the userer.
Dominican friars find a place for him in the palace of the
Marqueses de Madrigal, where he is given a little shop for
mending shoes in the doorway of the palace. Belarmino seems
completely happy. With his hermetic language he attracts students and professors to his shop, thus arousing the envy of
Apolonio, who sees no reason why such people should be so
attentive to this madman. He orders his son to pay no more
attention to Angustias, but, as his father is not very observing
of the reality about him, the friendship continues.

One day, the Duchess summons Guillén to her house to meet
the Bishop of the Diocese, once a cowherd for the Duke of
Somovia. Through the family's power, he has become a priest
and now an influential Bishop. The Duchess has similar plans
for Guillén, explaining her reasons that today "priests are the
men in Spain who count on the most flattering future." Their
humble origin does not matter. They will be received by the

best families, and the wealthy. Even if they are stupid, "politicians
and academicians will listen to them," and even if they are
homely, "the most beautiful women will look at them with
enchantment." The Duchess feels also that Guillén is honorable,
truthful, and has a good heart, "all of which is necessary to be
a charitable and worthy priest." (P. 77) Guillén enters the
seminary· at the age of fifteen.

Ayala now interrupts Don Guillén's history to turn his attention
to the philosopher and the dramatist, first pausing to comment
with ironic humor on the Marqueses de Madrigal, simple souls,
incapable of doing either good or evil, simply because of their
ignorance of the whole matter. They are convinced that heaven
is like a theater. God is, of course, the protagonist, and the public
are all saved souls, but there are social categories, the best seats
reserved for the highest, of which they feel themselves a prominent example. In a conversation with Padre Alesón, at one point
delightfully described as an "antediluvian pachyderm," they
express concern over Belarmino, who neglects his religious duties.
In the past, he violently criticized holy things, but now he seems
to do nothing.

Padre Alesón assures them that Belarmino will be saved. He
has declared himself a philosopher, and "a philosopher neither
hinders, nor molests, nor harms, as long as he is not taken seriously." (Pp. 80-81) Belarmino is no longer molested by his wife,
for she has become more domesticated and even somewhat
religious, since the Marqueses have forbidden her appearance
in his little shop. Angustias is very attentive to her father. Belarmino is happily proceeding with his philosophizing and his dictionary, or "cosmos." He comes across the word "camel" and en-
visions its stepping out with its humps and saddlebags. Henceforth, the "camel" is for him a minister of the Crown, and a
"dromedary" is a priest or minister of the Lord, because in each
case the hump represents responsibility.

The author expresses his concept of nicknames, which offer
either "a succinct biography or a picture in miniature," (P. 91)
applying this to Froilán Escobar who is called both the *Estudian-
tón* and the *Alligator*. The first, "a perennial student," reflects
Froilán's twenty years of study in the University. He is called
the Alligator because of his complete immobility during hours in
classes.

As Froilán and many others gather in rapt attention to hear the strange and fascinating discourses of Belarmino, Apolonio watches with ever-increasing envy and a desire for vengeance. He, too, must have a public success. Señor Novillo is a frequent visitor to Apolonio, both of them "recalling effigies of Buddha" with their size and shape. Apolonio has written an allegorical poem, a drama, which he wants presented to the public to win fame for himself. Novillo is more interested in watching from afar his beloved Felicita Quemada passing in the street than in what Apolonio has to say. Felicita is called *Quemada*, or *la Consumida* because she is consumed by the fire of love for Novillo, but nothing comes of their passion. She is a confirmed spinster and he a sentimental, elderly dignitary and town boss. Both are too timid to consider matrimony.

Urged on by Apolonio, the influential Novillo finally arranges for the presentation of Apolonio's drama by a company of comic actors which has come to town. They produce the drama, converting it into a farce, and the result is a huge success. Apolonio, always unaware of true reality, is delighted and becomes more and more careless of his duties as a shoemaker-artist. He feels that his success·has superseded that of Belarmino.

Meanwhile, a third shoemaker has come to town, who advertises in the newspapers and sells ready-made shoes. Apolonio is disdainful of such a travesty on art, but the Duchess warns him that, unless he applies himself to his business, he will go the way of Belarmino, and both will end in a charitable asylum.

As Apolonio is still engrossed in the success of his drama, he is suddenly confronted with a real-life drama. His son, called at this point in his youth Pedrito, sends him a note begging his pardon and explaining that he is eloping with the woman he adores. They plan to marry and hope for his blessing. Apolonio rushes to the Duchess with the letter. She tells him to sit down and assures him that this is nothing serious, his son has eloped with Angustias, the daughter of Belarmino. At this point, Apolonio feels himself truly a tragic actor and rises to say: "That no, that no! Rather death. . . . I was already disposed to pardon, to give my blessing. I even thought of the grandchildren. . . . But that, never!" (P. 120) This time he is too agitated to speak in verse.

The Duchess explains that the two had been meeting in the home of the romantic Felicita, who had helped them with their

elopement, but she herself will resolve the situation. She is
determined that there will be no wedding for Pedrito has a
beautiful future as a priest, and no future if he marries. The
Duchess finds out from Felicita where the pair have gone and
sends Apolonio, Novillo, and a strong-handed servant to bring
Pedrito home, while Angustias is left alone. Belarmino is crushed
at the news.

Felicita and Father Alesón are determined that the elopement
shall end in marriage, and the latter wins the support of the
Bishop. But the Duchess is a strong adversary and has a lively
dialogue with the Bishop, who acknowledges his debt to her but
refuses to act against his conscience. His final word is that the
marriage will be consummated unless God should impede it.
While the Duchess is no less determined, she recognizes that the
Bishop is a man of conscience, and she almost feels admiration
for him.

Meanwhile, Belarmino is consoled by an affectionate letter from
Angustias, wanting to come home, but Xuantipa had already an-
ticipated that and written her never to return, but to go hide
herself where no one will know her or her family. When Dominican friars go to seek her, she has disappeared.

The other love affair also has a sad end. Felicita has not seen
her beloved Novillo for days and finally is informed that he is
critically ill with pneumonia as a result of his night trip in the
rain to find Pedrito. Obliged to remove his false teeth and toupee
during his illness, he is too proud to see Felicita. He dies uttering
his last words of remorse for not having married her. She resolves
to enter a convent, first careful to inquire as to which Order has
the most becoming habit.

Pérez de Ayala has used Nature artistically in this chapter on
drama and philosophy in real life. During all the dramatic events,
it rains incessantly. Father Alesón has kindly deceived Belarmino
by telling him that Angustias is staying in a convent until her
wedding day. Belarmino, the devoted father, goes each day in the
rain to circle the convent and try to distinguish the sweet voice
of Angustias among those singing within. But he fails to hear her.

Then the rain ceased, and "it was the autumn season, the color
of honey and velvety silver mist like down, so that the earth
was like a ripe peach. Above the walls of the convent garden
appeared the black and rigid cypresses which were like the

prologue to a mystic rapture, . . . and the anemic and suffering willows . . . which were the weariness and exhaustion, sweet epilogue to mystic rapture. To the eyes, all was peace in the convent garden . . ." (Pp. 141-42)

The mist seems to penetrate the soul of Belarmino, and he is convinced that he has been deceived, that Angustias has not been in the convent, but that she is there now, seeking perfect serenity. The outer world is an illusion, and now for him there no longer exists Xuantipa, the userer, nor Apolonio and his son. He decides to abandon both philosophy and the mending of shoes.

Belarmino delivers a kind of final apologue to the Alligator to the effect that "once there was a man who, because of thinking and feeling so much, spoke little because he understood so many things in one single thing that he had difficulty in expressing himself. Others called him a fool." When he learned to express all these things, he spoke a great deal and was called a "babbler." Then he came to see in all different things a single thing, "because he had penetrated the meaning and truth of everything," and he remained silent. "And others called him a mad man." (P. 143) We note a quixotic quality in the apologue.

At this point, Don Guillén resumes his story, first reviewing his years in the seminary. His companions tended toward a life that revealed little vocation. Perhaps in reaction to this, Don Guillén became convinced that he had a great vocation for the priesthood. He was deeply moved by the music of the liturgy, perhaps at times too emotional. He learned Latin, studied French, and began English. His only distractions were study and reading, his favorite reading the hymns of the Breviary. He has become convinced that the Christian Church has been changing from a "spiritual power and apostolate of social charity" into a perishable "political power," losing thus "efficiency and stability." (P. 149) In contrast, the simple hymns of the Breviary please him as the reflection of innocent and pious souls of the early Church. He finds in them true Faith, Hope, and Charity.

The poetry and indescribable essence of the Breviary are to him the same poetry and essence of the soul of Angustias, and the "substance of poetry is, necessarily, love." In his seminary years, he felt a fear of darkness and a "desperate desire for light, warmth, love." (P. 152) After his fourth year in the seminary, he was convinced that he could best serve God by marrying Angustias, and in the home of Felicita he promised to marry her. There followed the elopement and its subsequent failure. After the disappearance of Angustias, the Duchess returned him to the seminary, and he spent seven more years studying for the priesthood, his love for Angustias still firmly rooted in his heart. He studied faithfully. Influenced by Saint Paul, he made a vow of chastity, feeling in his heart that any sin attributed to Angustias was really his sin for which he must atone.

After becoming a priest he served as chaplain for some time on the country estate of the now widowed Marquesa de Madrigal, and became interested in social problems and the happiness of these rustic people. The widow revealed to him one day that she was making him heir to her considerable wealth, which he agreed to accept only on condition that he use it for charitable purposes.

The Duchess of Somovia, before her death, arranged that he be made canon, and she asked him to do what he could for his father, Apolonio. Don Guillén brought his father to live with him, but the situation proved difficult, since Apolonio made love to the servants and even published a verse in the local newspaper declaring his love for the mayor's wife. He also ran up more debts than his son could pay. Consequently, he is now in an asylum, as is also Belarmino, now a widower. They have thus fulfilled the predictions of the Duchess of Somovia.

After the long recital of his story, Don Guillén turns to the picture of the beautiful girl on his desk. Though tomorrow will be Easter, he can never be happy, not knowing where she is. His listening friend arises immediately and tells Don Guillén once again that he knows the girl and can bring her here. In the café he finds Angustias and does as promised. The frightened Angustias, face to face with Don Guillén, her Pedrito of long ago, throws herself at his feet, asking pardon. Don Guillén kneels before her asking her pardon for all the sins for which he is really responsible. Thus they are briefly reunited, and a happy Easter will dawn. Don Guillén arranges that Angustias live with his best friend, an elderly and kindly canon, until further plans can be made.

The final scene is in the attractive garden of the asylum, on a beautiful Easter day. It is like a branch of the Rúa Ruera, for here live Belarmino, Apolonio, and the userer who lost his money in a bank failure. Felicita is also here as a nun. Then Colignon, the French confectioner, arrives with a large supply of fine pastries for his two old friends, who share them generously with their companions in the asylum.

Belarmino remains silent and aloof. Apolonio is still composing verses, this time to one of the nuns from whom he wishes a favor. He is on the point of concluding a drama which will bring fame and wealth. He still believes that he hates Belarmino, and he considers himself superior, having received an "academic education." To prove further his superiority, he always carries a bottle of Vichy water to his meals, as he has a delicate stomach.

Belarmino and Apolonio both receive telegrams from their respective children. Pedro Guillén has inherited the "fabulous fortune," and he will once more bring his father to live with him. Angustias is also saved by Pedro Guillén, who will bring her father to live happily with her.

Meanwhile, Apolonio has run out of authentic Vichy water and has gone to fill an empty Vichy bottle with water from a fountain, so that he may maintain his prestige by carrying the bottle in to dinner with him. He is discovered in the act by Belarmino, and is tempted to do away with his long-time enemy, once and for all. He overcomes the impulse, and instead, the two exchange the telegrams they have received. There follows a mutual embrace, silent, effusive, and fraternal, and a denial of any previous hatred or scorn. Apolonio says: "you are like my other half." Belarmino replies: "Yes, and you my other *testaferro (hemisphere).* (P. 186)

Belarmino has not abandoned his original language, nor has Apolonio abandoned his dramatic aspirations. Now he will write his great drama, inspired by Belarmino as Sophocles was inspired by Socrates. They are complementary halves forming a harmonious whole. They have discovered that love and friendship are the solution to their problems.

Froilán the Alligator died of hunger, as might be expected, leaving various valuable notes. In an Epilogue, the author expresses through these posthumous papers some of his own ideas on the philosopher and the dramatist. "The philosopher lives his own dramas; he is never a spectator." Hence, "he weeps within and smiles without," (P. 192) as does Belarmino with his

apparent indifference to the external world. His life is given over
to thought which he has great difficulty in transmitting with his
original and hermetic language. The dramatist, such as Apolonio,
spends his life in inventing and discovering dramas and expressing them objectively. Each needs the other as Belarmino and
Apolonio conclude in their final reconciliation.

Pérez de Ayala does not believe in absolute truth in worldly
matters. He believes that contrasting and opposing opinions may
each have some truth. He himself takes no side in the opinions of
the two shoemakers. He simply states: "Belarmino and Apolonio
have existed, and I have loved them." (P. 193) He does not
claim that they actually existed on this earth, but they existed
through him and for him. And: "That is everything. To exist,
multiply and love."

Pérez de Ayala has carefully constructed this novel both in
place and time. The first chapter occurs in the present, during
Holy Week. The following chapters go back into the past and
to the story of the two shoemakers and their children in Pilares,
partly told by the author-narrator, and in Chapters Four and
Seven by Don Guillén. The final chapter returns to the shoemakers on Easter Sunday in their asylum, looking forward to a
happy future, each with his own child.

Although some critics consider the characters to be largely
symbolic or even caricatures, we find them to be very real with
a whole gamut of human emotions, disdain, envy, ambition,
charity, and love, ranging from the frustrated love of Felicita
Quemada to the true love of Don Guillén, finally converted into
a love which is charity in his provision for Angustias. Sex does not
play an important role in the novel, and we may recall Don
Guillen's firm vow of chastity.

Frances Weber, referring to this novel in her study of Ayala,
writes: "The temporal frame of the novel is an impious inversion
of Christian symbol: the events leading up to the happy ending
of the love story take place during Holy Week; the prostitute
Angustias is restored to her lover, a priest, on Easter Sunday;
her redemption is accomplished through human, not divine
love."[6] We cannot agree with this interpretation. We find nothing
impious about this temporal frame. Angustias is not in effect
restored to "her lover, a priest." The fact that the two had
eloped some years before does not make him her "lover," and

Don Guillén has no intention of any such relationship with her or any other woman. He makes it clear at the beginning that she is now his sister. It can only be said that they were briefly reunited, but then separated permanently. Angustias and her father will live together. Divine love has wrought a change in Don Guillén and a firm vow of chastity in atonement for his responsibility for any sins which Angustias has committed. Divine love can be expressed through fraternal love. It is not a "happy ending of the love story," but a solution of the problems therein involved.

Ayala's ideas on religion and on priests have changed since the days of his attack on the Jesuits. The priests in this novel are Dominicans, and, for the most part, good men. There is sometimes in their presentation some humorous irony, so inherent in Pérez de Ayala. We feel that he is ironically humorous in laying down the reasonings of Don Guillén as to his disregard of the rules of abstinence during Holy Week. This is Don Guillén, the man, in the privacy of his room, not the priest, and while many would consider his eating meat on the occasion a sin, Ayala probably does not. We feel that Don Guillén was entirely sincere in his observations on the Breviary, reflecting the author's own appreciation of its beauty.

Another example of the good cleric is the Bishop who refused to yield to the demands of the vivacious Duchess, and insisted on maintaining his own views in accordance with his conscience. The other characters are well portrayed, such as the Duchess of Somovia, the delicate Angustias, the tyrannical Xuantipa, the inquiring Alligator, and others. In our opinion, Belarmino and Apolonio are not caricatures, for, while each lives outside reality in his own peculiar way, they are appealingly human in their moments of real crisis and emotion.

We repeatedly see the author's preoccupation with creative art, painting, drama, novel, and Belarmino's fascination with words and all their possible significance. An excellent study of the language of Belarmino has been done by Carlos Clavería.[7]

We cannot agree with Bernard Levy,[8] supported by Mary Ann Beck,[9] that critics have not been able to explain the philosophical implications of the novel because there are none. In our opinion, César Barja has explained well that in all of these last novels is presented the "fundamental problem of man's relation to the

Universe," and that in this novel "love is the formula of harmonious solution of the dialectic opposition between Belarmino and Apolonio." (P. 452) We should add to this the need and achievement of mutual communication and understanding.

Several critics have noted a relationship between this novel and *El Quijote*. Barja remarks that this novel "is the *Don Quijote* of this writer, perhaps of the Spanish contemporary novel." (P. 465) The French critic, Jean Cassou, writes that this novel "is certainly, after *Don Quijote*, one of the greatest Spanish books."[10] Leon Livingstone calls it "probably the finest modern example of the *Quijote*-type novel."[11]

To our certain knowledge, *Belarmino y Apolonio* has been translated to French, German, Italian, and Japanese. We have recently found reference to a translation of this complete novel into English.[12]

II *The Story of Urbano and Simona*

Following the publication of *Belarmino y Apolonio*, Pérez de Ayala continued with enthusiasm his fictional career. Since he had actually written this first major novel, with its Asturian setting, in a Castilian village, he was accused of not being able to see the Castilian reality about him. The author defended himself by noting that at the same time he was writing the long novel he also wrote a shorter work, now published as *Pandorga* (*OC*, II), which reveals his observations of the Castilian world about him at that time.

It is evident that shortly thereafter he spent some time in Portugal, for both parts of this bipartite novel recounting the story of Urbano and Simona are signed in Portugal, the first in September, the second in October of 1922. The two volumes were published in 1923.

A Luna de miel, luna de hiel (Honeymoon, Bitter Moon)

The first part of the novel about Urbano and Simona tends toward the expository, presenting characters and problems, while the second part contains more action and resolves the problems. The two-volume novel is divided into four parts corresponding to the waning and waxing of the moon. The first part, *cuarto menguante* ("waning moon"), opens in the home of Doña Micaela and her husband, Don Leoncio. They are seated at the table with their only son, Urbano, and his preceptor, Don Cástulo, who lives with them. Doña Micaela has announced the imminent marriage of Urbano to Simona, a girl of her choice, but Don Leoncio opposes the marriage as premature.

Urbano favors the idea of his marriage. He can now support a wife since he has been admitted to the practice of law, about which he knows very little. He has achieved admission with the help of Don Cástulo and also through the aid of his mother who used her influence with the examining professors.

Doña Micaela has two governing obsessions, one to make her son the perfect man, completely innocent and chaste until marriage, and the other, social ambition. Her husband is part owner of a local business, and she manages to associate with the "best people," among them the widow Doña Victoria de Cea, whose husband before his death had practically ruined the family fortune with his gambling. Doña Micaela is unaware of the depleted resources of Doña Victoria. This supposed wealth has been one of the reasons for her choice of Doña Victoria's daughter, Simona, as the ideal wife for Urbano. The two have actually loved each other in their innocent way since childhood.

Despite the protests of Don Leoncio, he is forced to accompany his wife to the country estate of Doña Victoria, now occupied by her mother, Doña Rosita, who inspires in Don Leoncio a desire to kneel before her. To him, she is a beautiful symbol of maternity. His ideal of woman is the mother, and as a result he allows himself to be dominated by the extravagant ideas of his wife, the mother of his son.

The betrothal is agreed upon, and the marriage takes place in the chapel of El Collado, the country estate, presided over by the widow's chaplain, a man of dubious character who travels about frequently with Doña Victoria. After the ceremony, Doña Rosita, who seems to have a power of divination, assures the young couple that they are now in "full honeymoon," after which comes the waning quarter.

One of the guests at the wedding is Paolo, a man of some fifty years, whose mother considers him too young for marriage, although he has been engaged for thirty-five years. He is devoted to riding horses and plays a rather important role later in the story.

The couple, innocent as the original Adam and Eve, go off on their honeymoon with the conviction that since they are married, they should both be happy. Therefore, each says aloud: "I am happy." Actually they are frightened, and Urbano wishes that bandits would hold them up and carry him off.

En route, Simona sees a cloud and is convinced that an angel of the Annunciation has brought her the news that she is to have a son, which pleases her very much. At their destination, they pass for brother and sister, and occupy separate rooms. Simona sleeps soundly all night, happy in her memory of the angel. Urbano sleeps not at all and finally resolves to go home, leaving his bride a note directing her to do likewise, and that they will see each other later.

Simona, on arriving home, finds only her grandmother, as her mother has gone off again with her chaplain. Simona is most unhappy. Urbano's arrival home produces considerable surprise, but his mother insists that he return at once to Simona, accompanied by his preceptor. Thus ends the quarter of the waning moon, with the comment by Don Cástulo: "Daphnis and Chloe alive again." (P. 68) It is obvious that Ayala is writing a modern version of the Greek story by Longus.

In the next quarter, the crescent moon, Urbano returns to Simona at the country estate, feeling a rebellion against his mother and a sense that she is to blame for his disquietude and unhappiness. Don Cástulo seems unable to help him, admitting to himself that this is what one would expect from the type of education Urbano has received and remarking to Doña Rosita that they are all characters of a farcical tragedy.

The young newlyweds, deeply in love, spend idyllic days together, wandering through woods and fields. Each sleeps in a separate room at night, but they meet on their adjoining balconies and discover the joy of innocent embraces and kisses, to the accompaniment of the song of the nightingale. Urbano longs for a fuller expression of their love but is confused and uncertain. He seeks an explanation from Don Cástulo, who gives him no specific answer, but advises him to observe nature and the animals, and to read books beginning with Genesis. Unfortunately, Urbano understands little of what he sees or reads. He is impressed, however, on reading that Adam and Eve were expelled from the garden.

Meanwhile, Doña Rosita's servant, Conchona, a healthy and primitive soul, has fallen in love with Don Cástulo, the classically erudite preceptor, and has no reticence in revealing it. He is drawn to her by her natural frankness, gaiety, rustic enchantment, and what he calls her moral beauty. They are a couple in striking contrast to the young newlyweds.

But at this point disaster arrives in the persons of a usurer and a representative of justice, who announce that the family must leave the property and all of its contents at once, since everything now belongs to the usurer. Doña Rosita has unfortunately given absolute power over all her property to her daughter, who had mortgaged everything and promptly spent the money with this result.

Doña Rosita is so shocked that she falls senseless, first declaring that she will never leave her home alive. Simona rushes to her side. Urbano observes the scene with a kind of intellectual curiosity, recalling what he had read of Adam and Eve and their ejection from the Garden of Eden. Conchona irately orders the two "vultures" out of the house, but Don Cástulo declares that they only represent the law, and he who speaks of law speaks of "injustice, brutality, misfortune." He tries to induce these men to suspend action for the moment and does achieve a brief respite. Meanwhile, Conchona revives her mistress with devoted and efficient care.

Doña Rosita can leave Urbano and Simona as an inheritance only her final words, declaring that this is a happy farewell. She is full of a celestial joy. They must not recall the beautiful gardens where they have loved as a lost Paradise, for the true "paradise is outside, beyond these walls, in the struggles of life." (P. 176) Although Doña Rosita's mind is clear as she gives her wise counsels, the kindly family doctor, who loves and respects her, declares her death imminent.

At this point, Doña Micaela arrives with firmly fixed plans. Since the marriage has not been consummated, such was God's will. There is in effect no marriage, and she has found out from a theologian that a divorce can be procured. She is determined to take Urbano and Don Cástulo home with her at once. Misfortune has come to their family, too. Her husband, after declaring himself bankrupt, has tried to commit suicide, and they must not leave him alone. While Don Cástulo protests leaving Doña Rosita when she is dying, he yields to the orders of Doña Micaela, and he and Urbano meekly accompany her home.

Before her death, Doña Rosita gives her granddaughter all her beautiful jewels, and, as if seeing into the future, advises her not to be impatient if Urbano delays his return for weeks or even months. She will always be what a wife should be, his slave, his lady, and his goddess, which nothing will destroy. She dies shortly thereafter with a vision of her Captain husband awaiting her in Paradise. Simona is consoled by the strong and kind Conchona.

B   Los trabajos de Urbano y Simona
(The Labors of Urbano and Simona)

The second volume of the novel continues the story. The title *Los trabajos de Urbano y Simona (The Labors of Urbano and Simona),* doubtless derives from the mythical "Labors of Hercules" and indicates the labors that Urbano and Simona will have to accomplish to make themselves worthy of true marital happiness. The first part of this volume is called "New Moon." Urbano is home in Pilares, and his mother takes him to arrange for a divorce, since she no longer desires the marriage, having heard of the loss of the estate. The priest is shocked at the amazing ignorance of Urbano, and finally reveals to him the facts of life, to which his first reaction is horror. The priest also explains in a pedantic manner the provision of canon law regarding marriage and divorce, but nothing is decided for the moment.

Meanwhile, Doña Rosita is buried in her bridal attire, and the grieving Simona goes to live temporarily in the humble, rustic home of Conchona and her numerous family. Don Cástulo returns shortly to make a formal request for the hand of Conchona, they are married within two weeks, and they are supremely happy. With the small capital which Don Cástulo has saved and with the ideas and energy of Conchona, they plan to set up an Academy to prepare students for more advanced studies. Urbano will be one of the professors. He is determined to make himself worthy of Simona and to be able to support her.

Simona also wants to make herself worthy, and to accomplish this she will suffer all the misfortunes necessary. She has already suffered the loss of her grandmother and her home, and the constant absence of her mother. In the final part of the novel, "Full Moon," we find that her mother has now forced her to live in Pilares with the seven spinster sisters of the priest, her constant companion. Doña Victoria has been informed that Urbano abandoned Simona after the seizure of the estate. Now she wants him never to return, and the seven sinister sisters are to guard her. They are envious of her beauty and good qualities, and do everything possible to make life miserable for her, but she bears it all with a smile. She wants to learn how to keep house, and she accepts their injustices cheerfully.

Urbano has discovered that Simona is in Pilares, and he wants to see her. His friend, Paolo, discovers that Simona goes out only to early mass, accompanied by the seven sisters. The two men follow them, and in mass Urbano and Simona exchange glances, only to be discovered by the sisters, who hastily escort Simona home. Urbano must talk to his bride, and this is accomplished through the machinations of Paolo's squire, a Don Juan type, who wins the favor of Trifona, one of the sisters. Trifona allows Simona to appear on the balcony on Christmas Eve, during the absence of the others at mass. The lovers talk, and Urbano is inflamed by the beauty of her voice. Through the same intermediary they exchange daily letters and finally achieve a meeting in the rear room occupied by Simona. Here Urbano becomes a man, and Simona becomes in fact his wife. But the sisters discover Urbano escaping by a rope. As a result, Simona is placed in the Convent of the Derelicts, also called the "Refuge of repentant maidens."

When the Mother Confident hears Simona's story, she can not understand why they have brought Simona here, for, since Urbano is her husband, she has nothing for which to repent. Simona explains that, before they can be united forever, they must pass through many labors. From her companions in the convent, Simona learns a great deal about life and love. She feels only pity for these unfortunates, reflecting the author's own attitude in this regard.

Through the arts of the Sister who serves as janitor, she receives daily letters from Urbano. It is the month of May, and all Nature is beautiful. Simona is supremely happy for she is now a woman and is going to be a mother.

Meanwhile, there is an epidemic of typhus, and several nuns

have died. Simona is tireless in her care of those who are ill.
Urbano, hearing of this, is determined to get Simona out of the
convent at once. Aided by Paolo and his squire, on the night of the
full moon, Urbano abducts Simona from the convent, and they
ride off to Conchona's home in the country. On arrival, Simona
is seriously ill with typhus, but in a few days she passes the
crisis and recovers.

As Baquero Goyanes points out, there are various details here
reflecting Cervantine influence.[13] The doctor orders that Simona's
hair be cut to relieve her in her delirium. As a result, she looks
like a young Adonis. However, she has not lost her beauty, as
did the maiden of *La española inglesa* of Cervantes. She travels
in the disguise of a boy, when the couple go off on their second
honeymoon, recalling the disguise technique used by Cervantes
in *Persiles y Sigismunda*, as well as by other authors of the
Golden Age.

On the original honeymoon trip, Urbano in his fright wished
that bandits would hold up the stagecoach and abduct him. On
this second trip, the stagecoach is held up by three bandits, but
Urbano's attitude has changed. He has learned fencing from
Paolo and boxing from his squire, and puts his skills to most
effective use in defending Simona and routing the bandits. He
is the hero of the hour.

Although Simona is disguised as a boy, they occupy one room
this time, and their happiness is complete, a happiness won by
their own sufferings and efforts. Balseiro considers that their
successful achievements have been won through two virtues, the
will of Urbano and the faith of Simona.[14] Urbano, with his
determination to learn about life's realities, has overcome his
mother's determination to keep him from a knowledge of these
things, when he finally rebels against her. His will to make his
own life with Simona is evident in his activities in the Academy,
in his attentions to Simona, his daily letters to her, and his final
abduction of her from the convent. Her faith in his love never
falters, and, as she suffers her trials, she is always convinced that
Urbano will come for her as her grandmother had prophesied
just before her death. Her faith in him gives her the power to
resist cheerfully all her trials and misfortunes.

Ayala some years before bitterly criticized Jesuit education. He
is now criticizing the lack of proper sex education in the society

of the day, but here his criticism is less bitter and much more artistically achieved. We have seen how the lack of knowledge along these lines resulted in considerable suffering for Urbano and Simona. But they finally develop through their efforts, faith, will, and love, into a real man and a real woman whose love will bear fruit in their child to come.

The author, speaking through Urbano, expresses his concept of woman in the latter pages of the second part of the novel: "The good woman, the one who fulfills her function and purpose, is no more than a woman; first sweetheart, then wife, then mother; the mother is the home. Man is sweetheart, husband, and father, by virtue of having been attracted by love." (P. 164) But to achieve his plenitude, he must be a man, face to face with other men and with nature. Urbano feels that Simona is "feminine perfection," and he hopes to be worthy of her as a man.

In accord with Ayala's interest in various perspectives on any problem, we find here variations of the problem of love and sex, portrayed in some characters who have somewhat abnormal aspects. Doña Micaela tries to dominate the lives of others with unfortunate results. She is cold to her husband, and when she later tries to rekindle his love and fails, she goes mildly insane. Her husband, Don Leoncio, disheartened by his wife's coldness, consoles himself with a mistress, but ultimately he finds that boring. Paolo is also a bit abnormal. In his fifties, betrothed for many years, he still lets himself be controlled by his mother, although he has a child out of wedlock.

Although there is great disparity in their background and education, Conchona and Don Cástulo are happy in their marriage. This erudite man has spent his life with the classics but is truly in love with Conchona, a child of nature, undisturbed by the facts of life, which seem to her perfectly natural. She brings her husband to see that truth is not only in books but also in the world about him. She is one of the most convincing characters in the novel.

The protagonists seem more like symbols than real persons in the early part of the novel, but not at the end. César Barja sums it up well: "A false education made of Urbano and Simona two children; love, sex, life, and nature make them man and woman, conscientious and responsible beings." (P. 464) The ignorance of Urbano and Simona at the beginning may seem implausible, but Ayala has probably exaggerated, particularly in the case of Urbano, in the desire to show the disastrous possibilities of such ignorance, and to make a plea for a more rounded education.

III *The Story of Tigre Juan*

After publishing the two-part story of Urbano and Simona (1923), Pérez de Ayala turned his attention to the short novels of *El ombligo del mundo* (1924), considered in an earlier chapter of this study. In this period, he was also writing for newspapers. Two years later his last great novel was published, the two-part story of *Tigre Juan* (1926). The two parts have divisions with musical headings indicating the movements in each. As Walter Starkie has pointed out,[15] it is a complete musical cycle like a sonata, with primary and secondary themes, moving now slowly, now rapidly, and with a final Coda.

A Tigre Juan (Tiger Juan)

This first volume of the novel has two movements: one "Adagio," or slowly, the other "Presto," or rapidly. The novel opens with a description of the market place, which is the "historic archive" of the town and its inhabitants. The square is surrounded by little shops selling an infinite variety of wares on Thursdays and Sundays, the town's market days. The other days of the week, most of the shops are closed, but not that of Tigre Juan, which opens daily and has a sign announcing his talents.

Tigre Juan is an amanuensis and a bloodletter. He writes letters and wills, he finds the best nursemaids, he is a homeopathic doctor with free consultations and economical medicines. He is a tall man with bronzed skin, a large head, shiny black mustache, thick, bushy hair, and a face both "barbarous and ingenuous." His nephew finds that he resembles Attila, the Hun. Tigre Juan goes out to the country every morning at dawn to gather herbs for his medicines, and spends the rest of the day at his post, where many people visit him in need of his talents. His real name is Juan Guerra Madrigal, but his nickname is Tigre Juan. People have given him the name because of a matter of honor. Tigre Juan loves children and is good to them, but they are afraid of him because of his fierce appearance.

He has few friends but very good ones, among them Nachín de Nacha, who comes to town on market days to sell hunting caps and talk with Tigre Juan. Another friend whom he admires is Vespasiano Cebón, a traveling salesman of silks and trimmings, who visits Pilares several times a year to sell his wares and tell fantastic tales to impress his hearers that he is a very successful Don Juan. Tigre Juan admires him because of his attractiveness to women, and hopes that he can avenge all the men who are deceived by women.

Tigre Juan delivers a long invective against women, calling them the vilest thing in creation. According to him, "Paradise was not lost only because of Eve. It is being lost every minute of the day and night through woman." (*OS*, p. 409)

Tigre Juan makes one exception to this. He greatly admires and respects Doña Iluminada, his neighbor in the market place, a widow of about forty. She is very much in love with Tigre Juan, but she realizes that he does not reciprocate her love. She seems to have powers of divination, a kind of intuitive perception as to what will be in the future, and also an insight into Tigre Juan's general feeling about women, attributing it to some cruel disillusion in the past, and, at the same time, a powerful longing for love which would lead to his marriage at some time in the future.

Meanwhile, Tigre Juan concentrates all his love on his nephew, Colás, actually not related to him and of uncertain parentage. Tigre Juan has raised him from a baby to manhood, and Colás now has only one term remaining to complete his course in law. However, he has fallen in love with Herminia, the granddaughter of Doña Marica, another shopowner of the market place. But Herminia rejects him for two reasons. She is frightened at living in the same house with Tigre Juan, and also she is more attracted to Vespasiano, the so-called Don Juan. Colás considers him effeminate. Rejected by Herminia, Colás joins the military service for overseas duty and leaves his uncle grief-stricken.

Tigre Juan would like to seek vengeance against Herminia for her rejection of Colás. Although he plays cards almost every evening with her grandmother, Doña Marica, and a clergyman, Don Sincerato, he has never especially noticed Herminia, who usually remained in a dimly-lighted corner of the room. On his next visit to their home, he sees Herminia by lamplight and is so startled he faints. She so much resembles his long-dead wife, Engracia, that he believes that she is the "resurrection of the flesh." This ends the first part, called "Adagio."

As to Engracia, she did not die by his hands. However, to protect the wife of her husband's superior officer, who had a lover, Engracia allowed the man to hide in her room, where he was discovered by Tigre Juan. Enraged, he started to choke her but stopped when she declared herself innocent. Engracia was ill after the attack, recovered, but died soon after. The experience has left a deep impression on Tigre Juan, for although she did not die as a direct result of his attack, he feels responsible for her death, and deep within him he is convinced of her innocence.

The second part of *Tigre Juan,* called "Presto," has more rapid action, following the slow movement in presenting the characters in "Adagio." Tigre Juan is a different man after his hallucination. Superimposed upon the memory of Engracia is the figure of Herminia, and he is in love with her. He longs to be like Vespasiano with his power to attract women. As he goes to the country in the early morning to gather herbs, he is drawn toward everything "by a kind of love, born of comprehension." He finds everything beautiful, useful, and good. (*OS*, p. 487)

In his longing to win her, Tigre Juan brings frequent little gifts to Herminia and her grandmother, and Herminia, with her feminine instinct, begins to understand the situation. When her grandmother urges her to accept him, the girl bursts into tears. She is afraid of him, but at the same time she is attracted by his strength and power. However, she is convinced that Vespasiano is the one she loves, and he is her means of escape, her longing for liberty. The author analyzes well her mental state and emotions, suggesting that her supposed hatred of Tigre Juan might indeed be a misunderstood passion of love.

B   El curandero de su honra (The Healer of His Honor)

The first division of the second part of the novel is also entitled "Presto." As the days, weeks, and months slip by from fall to spring, Herminia does not recall any specific request for her hand, but she finds herself officially engaged to Tigre Juan, without having been consulted. He is more and more conscious of his love for her, and Herminia remains serene, never forgetting the possibility of her escape with Vespasiano.

Vespasiano arrives several days before the wedding, and Tigre Juan, in his ingenious faith, urges the traveling salesman to call on Herminia, and, with his gift for making love, he must tell Herminia how much Tigre Juan loves her. Vespasiano makes the call, speaking of love on his own behalf. But when Herminia wants him to abduct her before the wedding, he reacts as the typical Don Juan with his double talk, assuring her that he will always carry her with him, in his heart. He finds the marriage a perfect arrangement, since he can then be her lover without any responsibility.

Shortly before the wedding, Tigre Juan plays the leading role in Calderón's *El médico de su honra* (*The Physician of His Honor*) in the local theater. In the play, the protagonist kills his wife who has presumably dishonored him, although she declares her innocence. Then he remarries. Juan plays the part with resounding success, and the audience looks at Herminia with a warning note in their glances. Vespasiano is present but leaves soon after, on the pretext that he has been called to Barcelona.

In another episode of the novel, the question of honor arises, and Tigre Juan handles it admirably. The officer's widow, whom Engracia had saved from dishonor in the Philippines, appears in the market place with her two daughters, declaring Tigre Juan to be their father. She must, therefore, prevent the wedding, since he has this prior responsibility. He does not fly into a rage, but handles the matter with coolness, denying any knowledge of her, and assuring her that she is either drunk or the victim of opium like so many Asiatics.

After the great theatrical success and his perfect handling of this false accusation in the market place, the market people give him a new nickname, "The Healer of His Honor." Now Herminia decides that she will marry him, and the wedding takes place with due solemnity.

Colás unexpectedly returns from his experiences overseas with a wooden leg. He is no longer interested in Herminia because he feels that any love she might now have for him would be pity or maternal love, and he responds to the news of his uncle's marriage to Herminia with congratulations. Colás soon falls in love with an attractive young orphan, Carmina, who lives with Doña Iluminada, and one day at dawn they go forth to fulfill their love and his ambitions as a traveling entertainer.

Their flight awakens in Herminia the urge to escape. On Vespasiano's next visit to town, Herminia takes command, telling him that she is ready to go away with him, and then she will be his. He tries various subterfuges to put her off, finally telling her that he has to go to Regium the following morning but will return in the evening. The following morning, Herminia joins him in the compartment on the way to Regium.

The following division of the novel is "Adagio." The lives of Tigre Juan and Herminia are now separated like a river that meets an obstacle and moves forward in two streams. In earlier editions of the novel the story of the two courses of their lives was printed in separate parallel columns on each page of the narration. Leon Livingstone comments on this "brilliant conception of dual but synchronized action," but finds it a "brilliant failure" because of the impossibility of reading two columns simultaneously.[16] It would seem that Pérez de Ayala came to the same conclusion, for, in the novel as it appears in his *Obras Selectas* (1957), there are no parallel columns. While their lives run parallel, the author narrates first the experiences of Tigre Juan and then those of Herminia.

"Thus Flowed the Life of Tigre Juan." (*OS*, 553-74). After he leaves Herminia in the early morning to gather his herbs, he feels a strange restlessness over the possibility of losing her. He wants above all to conclude his work on earth by leaving a son. On his return home, he finds Herminia absent, but Doña Iluminada assures him that she has gone to mass. She also indicates that Herminia is not well and is probably expecting a son. As Tigre Juan starts to seek his wife, he is met by Doña Marica who tells him that Herminia has disappeared with Vespasiano.

It is the Night of St. John, Tigre Juan's feast day. In his desperation, he goes to the mountains with Nachín, and here they watch the youths and girls love-making and dancing around the bonfires. To Juan, it is all like a dream, and he feels alone, dead, as Nachín tries to console and counsel him. In this dreamlike unreality, he hears the voice of Engracia saying: "Justice! I did not deceive you. You deceived yourself because you did not know how to love me enough." Then he hears the voice of Herminia: "Kill me if you dare." Again comes the voice of Engracia: "Healer of your honor: purge your own blood. Purify yourself." (*OS*, pp. 571-72) As Tigre Juan calls out the names of Engracia and Herminia, Nachín believes that he is the victim of evil spirits and symbolically baptizes him to drive them away. In the witchery of St. John's Eve, Juan feels that he has received a revelation, and knows what he will do. He will go home and await his wife's return.

Meanwhile, "Thus flowed the life of Herminia." (*OS*, pp. 575-95) On the train, Vespasiano urges her to go home at once. He insists that the essence of true love is liberty, and that there is no love but free love. He wants no obligations with Herminia. The author indicates the truly Don Juan-like character of Vespasiano through the words of Herminia: "Love frightens you, which, like death, stops and suppresses time. . . . You have never loved, nor will you ever be able to love. Your fate." (*OS*, p. 577)

Vespasiano piously declares that Juan is his friend, and he does not steal the wife of a friend. Herminia decides that, since she has left home with Vespasiano, she is a "lost woman." Vespasiano leaves her in a house of prostitutes which is familiar to him and later tries to see her there, but she locks herself in her room and refuses to see him. In the village the next day, she comes upon Carmina and Colás, who take her back to Pilares.

Doña Iluminada, convinced by Colás of Herminia's innocence, decides to defend her against the wrath of Tigre Juan, who has not yet returned from his visit with Nachín. The three of them take her home, where she is very ill. Tigre Juan, upon his arrival, is speechless, as Colás assures him of Herminia's innocence. Tigre Juan cannot communicate with words, and only hopes that his thoughts can be read by Herminia as he looks at her fixedly and declares mentally: "You have not dishonored me . . . I have dishonored myself with vengeful thoughts . . . Honor, I will give you complete satisfaction. With a man like me, there is no hesitation. The healer of his honor . . . But before, Herminia, I want to tell you that I adore you." (*OS*, p. 604)

At the same time, Herminia, her eyes fixed on Tigre Juan, is thinking: "Greater than the love you had for me is that which I now have for you; now that I am your dishonor and abhorrence. Death I deserve," but not yet. She wants to live long enough to give life to their son. (*OS*, p. 604-5)

Tigre Juan silently withdraws. When they find him, he is seated, practising his art of bloodletting upon himself. He has written a will, leaving everything to his adored wife. It is his

wish that no one be blamed for his death. He is dying for his
own crimes about which no one knows nor can presume to know.
Herminia takes him into her arms as if trying to transmit to him
her life, begging that he be saved. Convinced of her love for him,
he stops the hemorrhage. The scene is well and convincingly told.

The novel is closed with a "Coda" to complete the story. A
beautiful son is born to them. When the baby is three months
old, they make a trip to Madrid to please Herminia, Juan proudly
caring for the baby on the train. As the thoughts and sentiments
of Juan are too ineffable for prose, the author closes the novel
with these thoughts, expressed in poetry:

> Our Father, who art in Heaven!
> My son, who art in my arms!
> My wife, who art by my side
> And flesh of my flesh, and we are
> Body and soul, you and I, in this son of ours!

> (*¡Padre nuestro, que estás en los cielos!*
> *¡Hijo mío, que estás en mis brazos!*
> *¡Mujer mía, que estás a mi vera*
> *y en mi tuétano estás impregnada, y estamos*
> *alma y cuerpo, tú y yo, en este hijo de entrambos!*) (*OS*, p. 624)

He speaks of the swiftness of life and its mystery which we
shall never fathom and concludes:

> To live to dream. Life is a dream.
> We mortal men do not dream.
> We ourselves are a dream.
> The world is the dream of God.
> Dream of love. Sublime mystery.
> My son, who art in my arms!
> My wife, flesh of my flesh!
> Our Father, who art in heaven!

> (*Vivir. Soñar. La vida es un sueño.*
> *No soñamos los hombres mortales.*
> *Nosotros mismos somos un sueño.*
> *El mundo es el sueño de Dios.*
> *Sueño de amor. Sublime misterio.*
> *¡Hijo mío, que estás en mis brazos!*
> *¡Mujer mía, impregnada en mi tuétano!*
> *¡Padre nuestro, que estás en los cielos!*) (*OS*, p. 626)

This is the end of the novel, but the author seems to feel that he has left some things unsaid, and he adds a "Parergón" or accessory document to cover the lapse of time between the attempted suicide of Tigre Juan and the birth of his son. He explains that in this tragicomedy the characters "had to pass through a period of elimination of passions and reflections upon themselves." (*OS*, p. 627) Seeking their own expression of their very essence, they delight in long discussions in which there is no clash of emotions, but a contrast of ideas.

Tigre Juan, recovered from his loss of blood, spends his days at his work in the market place, his head held high, as a challenge to what anyone may say. Colás is still insistent on free love and no marriage under the laws of Church and State. The author expresses his opinions on this matter and love and honor in general through the words of Tigre Juan in his discussion with Colás. Juan believes that honor is supreme liberty, the sense of one's own God-given responsibility. "Honor is faithfulness to one's self and bravery to face the consequences of one's own actions." (*OS*, p. 632) Free love is liberty without responsibility.

Love and desire are born together, according to God's will that man propagate life, but, when desire is satisfied, love remains and "has its satisfaction in itself, and continues in man's love for his wife and children." If man penetrates "the true essence of honor, he will remain faithful to his love in the cruelest vicissitudes," and this is matrimony. A single union based on these principles justifies "a divine law to sanctify it and a human law to exalt it, as if God and men were all witnesses of this step, honorable and sublime." (*OS*, II, 633)

Moreover, if a single soul feels closer to God in the shadow of the naves of the cathedral, the cathedral's existence is justified. Ayala goes farther to say that if a single Jew, Turk, or Lutheran is sincere in his religious desire, there is justified in his city a synagogue, a mosque, or a Protestant house of worship. Also, if a man is moved by Christian principles, but does not practise his faith, he is setting a bad example. As a result of their lengthy discussions, Colás and Carmina are married by both Church and State.

Pérez de Ayala turns also to his Don Juan theme in a conversation between Colás and his uncle. It is rumored that Vespasiano is returning to town. The two agree that Vespasiano is a Don

Juan and that all Don Juans are traveling salesmen, dealing in
trimmings, silks, and novelties. Don Juan is a half-man. He has
mistaken his reason for being and has never left in the world
surviving sons nor works. But in the theater he ended by going
to Heaven. Of course, this is not true in the original Don Juan
play by Tirso de Molina, but it is true in *Don Juan Tenorio* by
Zorrilla. The author, through Tigre Juan, expresses the opinion
that "God is, besides being infinitely just, infinitely merciful . . .
and that in the Final Judgment, all the creatures of God will be
saved." (*OS*, p. 649)

Tigre Juan plans to treat Vespasiano with indifference and
scorn, for to treat him otherwise would be equivalent to admitting
that he is a rival. Vespasiano comes to see Tigre Juan, who embraces him with such a crushing embrace that he almost cracks
his ribs. He remarks: "You are a part of myself which is lacking
in me; as I should be a part of you." (*OS*, p. 651) But such an
interchange is impossible. Half angrily, half humorously, he
scorns Vespasiano as a deficient and impotent Don Juan, and
then he invites him to his home to see Herminia. He has learned
to have faith, but Vespasiano does not accept his invitation.

The novel is well structured with the themes of love and honor
interwoven in a musical cadence, now slow, now fast. The characters are convincingly portrayed through description, dialogue,
and varied perspectives. The virile Tigre Juan is in striking contrast to the effeminate Vespasiano. The changing psychology of
Tigre Juan is well expressed in his contrasting surnames, Guerra
Madrigal ("War Madrigal"). He is warlike in appearance and
his impulsive bursts of temper, but all this covers a poetic and
sentimental nature that longs for love. He attacks women at the
beginning of the novel because he has not recovered from his
early marital experience, but at the end he has reversed his
opinion, having found the satisfaction of true love. Another well-
done psychological study is that of Herminia, as her feeling for
Tigre Juan develops from fear and hatred to a deep love. The
remaining characters who form the world of the picturesque
market place in Pilares are live people possessing normal human
virtues and weaknesses.

IV Justicia (Justice)

Besides these novels, Ayala wrote one last bit of fiction, *Justicia*

(Justice), 1928, found only in his *OC,* II, a short novel of some forty pages, which begins on a lyric note, the musical sounds of a smithy. But the lyric note soon changes to the dramatic, and there follows the story of the brutal murder of the five women of his household by the blacksmith to free himself from their tyranny and bigotry. Justice is sought, and the murderer, talking like a psychopath, declares his innocence. He is nevertheless duly tried, given five death sentences due to the ardent prosecutor, and executed, to the satisfaction of the townspeople who do not believe in the defense that he was a pathological idiot, and therefore society was responsible. After his death, his soul was seen in a cloud ascending to heaven.

A violent and damaging hurricane follows the execution. The prosecutor and townspeople are terrified at this manifestation. Perhaps this was not justice after all. Justice is viewed from various perspectives such as God's justice, man's hunger for justice, public justice, with a frequent note of irony. The reader is left to draw his own conclusions. This last short novel shows Ayala's continuing preoccupation with justice, in a plot rather strange to his fiction, but not to his concern with the problems of mankind.

V Conclusion

Pérez de Ayala wrote in *Las máscaras:* "Works of art are real or not, by virtue of a rare gift with which the true artist is endowed, and not because they are like or unlike the model imitated." (*OC,* III, 188) He believes that artistic reality is achieved by "creating an imagined world and giving it reality." (*OC,* III, 190) That is just what Ayala has done in his major novels; he has created an imagined world and given it reality. The very real setting in all of them is Pilares (the author's native Oviedo), and its environs. The characters fit well into the setting, but their characteristics and problems are largely universal.

Referring once more to the Prologue to the Losada edition of *Troteras y danzaderas,* we may recall that Ayala said there that in these novels his purpose was to recreate in the present "some of the eternal norms and vital values." (P. 19)

Love is an eternal norm and a basic theme in these novels. In *Belarmino y Apolonio,* the normal love between man and woman is frustrated. The love of Don Guillén and Angustias is frustrated by paternal intervention; that of Felicita and Novillo by a psychological problem, a fear of marriage. Paternal love is strong in both Belarmino and Apolonio, and filial love in their children. Brotherly love triumphs, as Belarmino and Apolonio are united at the end.

In *Luna de miel, luna de hiel* and its sequel, the protagonists suffer from an inadequate education necessary to a normal marriage, finally achieved through their own efforts. The parents of Simona are unhappy in their marriage, due to the character of Simona's mother. The love of Conchona and Don Cástulo is a happy, healthy love.

In *Tigre Juan* and its sequel, love is presented in various aspects. The true passion of love is achieved by the main protagonists and by Carmina and Colás. Doña Iluminada's love for Tigre Juan is expressed in unselfish devotion and practical help. Vespasiano is a weak Don Juan, whose attentions to women have a serpent-like quality. Paternal love is strong in Tigre Juan, both for Colás and for his own son. It is a tender love which is his very essence, in striking contrast to his external appearance.

The author's love for his *patria chica* is evident in his beautiful portrayals of his native Asturias, in all of these novels. But they are not mere paintings of scenes and customs. His characters have universal problems, which they work out in this background. We may recall Belarmino outside the convent, seeking for Angustias, with nature corresponding to his mood. The love of Urbano and Simona is developed in the idyllic setting of the country estate. Tigre Juan loves nature in his early morning trips to seek herbs. Nature plays an important part in all of these novels.

Ayala's love of his country is evident in his preoccupations for Spain. He seeks vital ethical values such as justice, which he finds too often unfair, due to dishonesty and bribery. He seeks honor which is integrity, honesty to one's self, which has little to do with the time-worn code of honor. He believes in freedom, but freedom with responsibility, and tolerance is important to him.

Intellectual and philosophical speculations are prominent in these novels as in most of Ayala's writings. He continues to seek man's relationship to God and to the Universe, and in these more mature products of his art, he appears to solve the problem more satisfactorily than in his early poetry, as he speaks through

Don Guillén of the church as a spiritual community supported by mutual love. Tigre Juan, in his poem, refers to the world as "the dream of God, a dream of love" and a "sublime mystery." While he does not understand the mystery, he seems to have faith in God.

Ayala deplores the thought that the Church has become a political power, thus lessening its spiritual power. He is less anticlerical as he portrays many good priests in these novels. He has not forgotten, however, that there are too many priests who enter the clergy without vocation, as a way of life, according to Don Guillén's observations in the seminary, and too often a priest's advancement depends on the influence of his wealthy and powerful friends.

These novels have a true aesthetic value. Ayala seeks beauty and finds it, sometimes in the most unlikely places. We may recall the dual description of the Rúa Ruera, which gives the reader an artistic vision of the street. The author has an excellent sense of proportion, and there is balance and rhythm in his prose. He likes to portray scenes and characters, often in contrast, as has been pointed out by Baquero Goyanes and others. These changing perspectives add greatly to the effectiveness of the novels which have frequently amusing and ironic complexities. In these novels, Pérez de Ayala has achieved the "universal harmony of the eternal norms and vital values" which he sought.

CHAPTER 6

Nonfictional Prose

AFTER completing the major novels we have discussed, and the short novel *Justicia*, the latter somewhat related in characters and setting to the short novels of *El ombligo del mundo*, Pérez de Ayala abandoned his creative writing. The reason for his abandonment of fiction is not definitely known, but it is certain that during this period he was deeply concerned with the political and social problems not only of Spain but of Europe. There is also an indication that he could better his economic situation by his contributions to newspapers. He affirmed that the closest solution to the author's economic problems was offered to him by journalism. *(Divagaciones,* p. 317)

The history of Ayala's nonfictional writings goes back to his childhood in Oviedo when his interests along these lines were already awakening. According to the earlier mentioned article by Manuel Fernández Avelló, Ayala's first journalistic writings were published in the liberal newspaper of Oviedo, *El progreso de Asturias.* Then he and his young friends founded their own weekly periodical, *El leño (The Log),* the title taken from the nickname of a young baggage porter of Oviedo. As a nickname "Leño" has the connotation of dull or thick-witted. In any event, Ayala contributed various satirical articles to this publication, and his articles were probably not dull.

Also, his father was very fond of cockfights and possessed his own cockpit. His son shared his father's enthusiasm and wrote articles on cockfights, half in prose and half in poetry, for a local publication devoted to the subject. For these contributions, the youth used the pseudonym of "Torquemada," a name famous in the history of the Spanish Inquisition.

It was somewhat later that Ayala collaborated with Juan Ramón Jiménez and others in *Helios,* contributing not only poetry and short stories but various articles of literary criticism. After the publication of his first volume of poetry and his first novel, he wrote regularly for the major newspapers of Spain and later of Mexico and South America. He occasionally signed his name as "El Claviero" or one who "puts on the screws."

Ayala was a prolific nonfictional writer, his articles and essays numbering between nine hundred and one thousand, now available in some fifteen volumes, thanks to the tireless labors of J. García Mercadal. There are doubtless many more as yet uncollected. A limited number of his most interesting and outstanding nonfictional writings is chosen here for consideration.

I *Ayala's Ideas on Journalistic Writing*

On several occasions Ayala has written about the importance of journalistic writing. In an undated essay on "El periodismo literario" in *Divagaciones literarias (Literary Musings)*, 1958, the author explains his attitude. As he writes, he feels that he is maintaining a conversation of immeasurable scope with all the invisible friends that are his readers. (P. 275) He is very much interested in the replies of the readers as a means of evaluating himself. When a person from Buenos Aires upbraided him severely because in a single Ayalan article the reader had to consult the dictionary six times, he was doubtless pleased.

Most of his writings for newspapers are not mere journalistic reports but literary essays. In an article dedicated to Gregorio Marañón, in 1926, Pérez de Ayala defines the essay specifically, as he writes: "In every model essay, more or less clearly and above the impressions of a literary nature, the author offers himself to us under a double aspect: as an intimate man and as a mirror of the universe. The essay is the most personal literature, the most closely bound to the person of the author. An essay is worth exactly what the man is worth who has written it (after living it and thinking it)." (*Amistades*, p. 230)

While Spanish Ambassador in London, Ayala pronounced a discourse on "Journalism and Diplomacy" (1932) before the Association of the Foreign Press, expressing his ideas and ideals regarding the two. He feels that both fields involve a tremendous responsibility. The journalist does not merely produce information, but "he must try by means of exact information to achieve the greatest and most intimate comprehension among nations.

Comprehension consists in an act of justification of one's neighbor." Being more comprehensive, we can justify the greatest number of differences among us. Both proper journalism and diplomacy should lead to an understanding among men and nations to produce universal harmony, which is the underlying philosophy in Ayala's writings. (*Amistades,* pp. 309-17)

II   *Ayala's Interest in England and the United States*

Some of Ayala's earliest articles now available in book form are found in the first half of the volume *Tributo a Inglaterra (Tribute to England),* 1963, a collection of essays reflecting the author's interests and observations during his stay in England from April to December, 1907, and published regularly in *El Imparcial* of Madrid, the same year.

After spending some three months in England, Ayala comments that he has seen many things, but not the sun. He humorously observes that while the sixteenth-century King Charles of Spain, commonly referred to as the Emperor Charles V of the Holy Roman Empire, could well say that the sun never set on his empire, the British Sovereign, Edward VII, could affirm that the sun never shines on his kingdom. (Pp. 105-6)

His declared purpose in these articles on England is to examine diligently "the qualities that throughout history have made of this people the greatest and most powerful of all that today exist and to select from them those which transplanted to Spain might take root in the soil of our temperament and be cultivated with success." He recalls with great consolation the words of Montaigne, that "Providence has conceded force to the men of the North, creative talent to those of the South." He is convinced that a "well-established gymnasium, individual and collective, physical or intellectual," could make the Spaniards as strong as the English, and he adds "and, of course, much more intelligent." (P. 106)

He enjoys the British Derby and the Regattas, and he is an admirer of British sports, especially football. He has read with enthusiasm that provision has been made for organized games of cricket, football, and hockey for both young boys and young girls, and is convinced that valuable ethical lessons can be learned from sports, and especially football, such as "the mechanism of play, 'the give and take,' loyalty to comrades, one's own renunciation before a common cause, the pride in others' triumphs, the acceptance of victory with modesty, defeat with the proper composure, and finally the acquisition of the spirit of discipline, of a corporate life, and of innocent and healthy enjoyment." (P. 129) Since that early day, football has gained a strong hold in Spanish life.

Ayala admires the feminine beauty and elegance to be found in Hyde Park and Covent Garden, but is concerned about the economic expenditures of some of these ladies. However, one of them suggests that their expenditures enable many other families to live. He is also intrigued by English beggars who, according to him, wander about reciting Shakespeare.

Little escapes his eye or his mind. He reflects on various scientific experiments, on the evils of alcohol, and at the same time he blessed absinthe for having inspired some of Verlaine's best poems. With a sense of humor he comments that a recent Congress in London has discussed alcohol, but one brave member defends it from the accusation that it causes cirrhosis of the liver, for this doctor has found cats with cirrhosis of the liver, and he believes that cats are abstemious. (P. 169) In the same vein he notes that in Cambridge, there is an Esperanto Congress, but meanwhile, God listens to prayers in many languages and responds with works, not Esperanto. (P. 171)

He contrasts the House of Lords with the Commons, the former secure in its long tradition of conservatism which will overcome the noisy House of Commons with its variable liberalism. He admires the Royal Family and describes the visit of the Spanish Royal Family to England, where they were enthusiastically received both in London and on the estate at Sandringham, at the time belonging to the Prince of Wales.

Although it was well before World War I, there are speculations as to the strength of Germany and as to whether she could land troops in England and overcome the country. This subject occupies more and more of Ayala's attention as time goes on. Meanwhile he remarks that "history is a dizzy race of ups and downs. . . . The English are pround of what they are; the Germans for what they will be. We Spaniards can be proud of what we have been." And he concludes: "England has fulfilled a great civilizing mission." (P. 253)

The articles of the first half of this volume were interrupted by the tragic death of Ayala's father and the necessity of his immediate return to Spain. The second half of the volume, dealing with both British and other subject matter, was written some years later, in 1938 and 1939. One of his literary studies is a comparison of John Bunyan's *Pilgrim's Progress* and Cervantes' *Don Quijote,* and Ayala concludes that in both works "children delight and men learn." He considers them supreme in the "density of their substance, both divine and human." (P. 269) Other later essays have to do with a variety of subjects, including a few on the War and the European crisis.

Another foreign country attracting Ayala's great interest was his wife's native land, the United States, especially during his trip there in the fall of 1913 for the occasion of his marriage to Miss Mabel Rick, and also during a second visit to the United States, in 1919-1920. The articles written during these years for newspapers in Spain and Buenos Aires have appeared in book form with the enticing title, *El país del futuro (The Country of the Future),* a title, according to Ayala, borrowed from the English writer, James Bryce. As in his essays on British life, in this collection dedicated to the United States, Ayala declares a similar purpose to transmit to his pages "everything seen or suggested which he thinks may be exemplary or of benefit to Spain." (P. 17)

Ayala considers that there are three aspects of special interest in a political state: first, its federal and local government, with its structure and mechanism, which can best be studied in books devoted to the subject; second, its political parties, which are very pronounced in the United States; and third, the public opinions which have engendered these parties and their struggles. He calls "public opinion the Holy Spirit of the true democracy." Besides these forces so determining to the political state, there are "certain intellectual and spiritual forces which create the family, religion and art," and to these he will give most attention. (Pp. 20, 21)

He refers to the United States as "the country of maximum and continuous effort," (p. 43) but while he is interested in its rapid growth, its inventions, and its wealth, he is not especially impressed by its great cities with their skyscrapers. The mechanical and material achievements are doubtless important, but he still adheres to his basic philosophy, as he writes: "I do not look with intimate reverence at anything but the creative act of the intelligence—knowledge—and the creative act of the will—ethics; or said in one word: culture. I am not stirred, nor moved, nor exalted except by Beauty, Truth, and Good." (P. 155)

He is delighted by Allentown, Pennsylvania, with its tree-lined streets, like avenues, and its individually owned homes and gardens. During the day, the streets are full of traffic and activity, but he is impressed by the fact that the inhabitants are in bed by midnight. All is quite different from his native land.

On his second trip to the United States, following World War I, New York was alive with the activity of returning troops, and he missed the peacefulness of his earlier visit. In these later essays, he is amused at the views of the various newspapers and the declaration by each that without its own country's intervention World War I would have been lost. He is waiting for some foolish newspaper to declare that Germany won the war.

Writing of sports, he includes an essay comparing fair play in boxing and bullfighting, concluding that the latter is less cruel. He also points out that while various men fight one bull in the ring, in other sports elsewhere various men also go after one fox or one lion. The fox and the lion are likewise at a disadvantage. The grace and plastic beauty of a man facing a bull have far more aesthetic appeal than that of two ponderous men trying to knock each other out in the boxing arena. The presence of potential tragedy also adds to the emotional effect of the bullfight. (Pp. 217-20)

In the year 1920, the United States was seething over the Prohibition law which seemed to assume greater importance than the League of Nations. Ayala views the situation with objective equanimity, and reports on the eve of the last day of free intoxication: "Two cities above all felt themselves possessed of a bacchanalian delirium: Washington, the official and political capital of the Republic, and New York, the financial and social capital, because the United States is bicipital, it has two heads, and that night it lost the two heads." (P. 254) He has observed and quotes accounts from the newspapers, but he does not try to make judgment as to whether alcohol is good or bad. He remarks that normally the laws are complied with in the United States, but immediately after Prohibition countless means were devised to evade the law. Only the truly wealthy were able to circumvent it. Meanwhile, it has been a tremendous expense to the country to try to enforce this law.

Ayala disagrees with those who disparage the United States because it had no history. In reality, history is "the known past," or the known past "lived in the present." His theory recalls Ortega y Gasset as he remarks that "all things aspire, consciously or unconsciously, to their maximum expansion, to their full realization. This is the meaning of the philosophy of history; this is the meaning of civilization; this is the meaning of life." (P. 90)

Pérez de Ayala considers the United States as the country which has the greatest capacity for future expansion. Among other things, the country has a long history of inventions which have contributed to the conquest of time and space, and for which other countries may be grateful. Ayala mentions among other "little things," as he calls them, the American inventions of the cotton gin, the sewing machine, the telegraph, and the telephone, and he pays tribute to their inventors, who he believes invented these things not motivated by a desire for personal gain, but for the general good.

As for wealth in the United States, it is impressive and should serve as a factor in the solution of social problems. He feels that half of the famous fortunes of such families as the Rockefellers and others should belong to the citizens of New York, since their original investments have achieved fabulous growth concurrently with the growth of that state.

Ayala is interested in the labor problems of the United States, the frequent strikes, the American Federation of Labor, and the views of many Americans that labor is asking too much; but when the Americans compare financial facts in Spain with those in the United States, the Americans always give many statistics in defense of their own country and conclude that Spain is backward.

Writing in 1920, Pérez de Ayala seems to have the gift of looking into the future, as he remarks that at that time "North American public opinion sees the Bolshevik cloud not just as a shadow on the line of the horizon, but rather as a dark cloud, pregnant with lightning, which covers the whole firmament." (P. 334)

After all the political and social observations regarding *El país del futuro*, Ayala closes with an essay expressing joy at being back in Spain, traveling on a slow train from Cádiz to Sevilla, where he has time to enjoy the charming countryside of his native land.

III Hermann, encadenado (Hermann, in Chains)

In the summer and fall of 1916, between his two visits to the United States, Pérez de Ayala was invited by the government in Rome to visit the Italian war front, and his chronicles were sent by daily cable to *La Prensa* of Buenos Aires, for which he was war correspondent. While these were written as newspaper articles, many of them are more literary than journalistic in nature. They were first published as a book in 1917, with the title *Hermann, encadenado (Hermann, in Chains)*.[1] They are now available in his *Obras selectas*[2] from which we shall quote. Early in the book, the author explains the title: "In the year 9 of our era, the Emperor Augustus sent the Latin proconsul Quintilius Varus to fight against the Germans, led by Arminius. The Roman general was defeated, and Rome was losing the hope of dominating Germany." (*OS*, p. 989) But after twenty centuries, the reincarnation of the former Quintilius Varus is achieving a complete triumph over Arminius, "subjugating and enchaining him forever." In other words, Italy is now achieving revenge for not having impressed Latin culture on Germany in the past. Anticipating the coming victory, the Italians now have Hermann, the modern version of the ancient German, Arminius, in chains.

The author describes these articles as travel notes written in haste, recording what his senses perceived, and the resultant ideas that came to him. It was his third trip to Italy, "the land of beauty," and also "of liberty." He reviews the glories of its history of achievements, maritime and artistic, its aristocracy of ancient lineage, and its world conquests.

Always with an artistic appreciation of architecture, Ayala admires even some of the Italian railroad stations, such as the stations of Turin, Rome, Milán, and Genoa, and naturally also the beautiful Gothic cathedral of Milán.

Despite the daily horrors of his visits to scenes of war, he describes many beautiful landscapes. He remarks that when one examines Italy "from the South to the North, one believes that God has modeled this peninsula lovingly with his thumb from yielding and pleasant material, like a sculptor in love with beauty. But then, the Supreme Maker, tired of such intense and exacting labor, began to form the Alps with blows from his fists . . ." (*OS*, p. 1025) Thus we see the contrast between the soft beauty of the South and the ruggedness of the North.

Not only did Ayala see the beauties of Italy but also the horrors of the battlefield. He visited various battle fronts, he saw corpses half-buried, their forms outlined beneath the surface, shoes rising into the air. He saw severed members, dried and mummified. (*OS*, p. 1051) On the Carso, the land seemed to be like a petrified sponge filled with blood and never tired of drinking more, and above the land was a reddish vapor rising toward heaven. (*OS*, p. 1033) The author could witness all these horrors, and then turn to the beauties of Italy, again revealing his great ability at contrast.

His trip to Venice recalled his first visit there with a small group among whom was the young lady to whom he now refers as "The great love of my life." (*OS*, p. 1153) He was saddened then because they were to have a long separation before their marriage. He is saddened now by the Venice of war and mourning.

His love of Italy is apparent in this book, his love of the beauty of her landscape as well as his great knowledge of her rich history and culture. His erudition is evident in his constant natural references to great Italian writers and artists, and to other great world writers. It is a charming book which deserves far more attention than it has received.

IV *Other Writings on War and Politics*

While *Hermann, encadenado* had as its content the chronicles of a war correspondent, and they are excellent chronicles, it is the aesthetic and literary values of the book that seem to us more important today. Some time before this volume on Italy and the War, Ayala wrote a series of articles for Madrid newspapers, collected also by J. García Mercadal and published under the title *Tabla rasa* (1963). They cover the period from 1913 to 1917. The title is difficult to translate satisfactorily, but the author explains that he chose it as signifying something like the old Roman custom of pleasant conversation after the meal was finished. Thus it can mean the "Table Cleared."

As the period covers the years leading up to and beginning the First World War, Ayala discusses the attitude of other nations, such as the United States, which regarded the war as the end of royalty and the coming of republics throughout Europe, believing that European civilization had proved itself a failure.

While he feels that the classification of the Germans as barbarians has been exaggerated, it is obvious that Germany is fighting for expansion and is stimulated by material ideals. He is convinced that the cause of the Allies is just, they are fighting the historic continuity of their spiritual tradition, and they are stimulated by high ideals. "It is the eternal struggle between greed and the instinct of conservation."[3] He repeatedly affirms that the Allied cause is just and will win.

The volume *Pequeños ensayos (Little Essays)*, 1963, contains a group of articles written between 1914 and 1919, but they are rather journalistic in nature, often reporting what has been said elsewhere about the War. At the beginning of both 1917 and 1918, he asks hopefully if this will be the year of the longed-for peace. However, he is optimistic that there is an obvious moral progress in the world, because every one speaks of the horrors of this war as the worst ever experienced. In his opinion, the horrors are the same as in former wars, but man is now more shocked by them. This is evidence of his moral improvement. (P. 126)

In 1918, Pérez de Ayala published his volume of essays *Política y Toros (Politics and Bulls)*, thus discussing two leading subjects of coversation among Spaniards. There seems to be considerable confusion as to the original date of the book's publication. Even Pérez de Ayala at one point refers to it as 1920, later correcting himself. As confirmation of the correct date, we have in our possession the original edition with the biographical data clearly indicated as Madrid: Ed. Calleja, 1918. The section on politics was written in 1917. The work is also found in Ayala's *OC*, III, and in his *OS*.

The author explains in the Prologue to his first edition, which serves as an *Apéndice* to the much enlarged version of the work found in his *OC*, III, that if he lived in a civilized country such as France, England, or the United States, he would have dedicated himself to a specialized and absorbing activity: art, science, industry. But in Spain it is impossible; he is too concerned with its politics. His specific preoccupations here are, first, the European war, and, second, the fact that Spain has not felt itself obligated to enter into this war for civilization, for it lacks a political conscience and is not yet a civilized nation. Her "citizens do not enjoy liberty of spirit or strength of will." A civilized nation must have "a minimum of political ideas common to all citizens, and then some margin of disparity." (*OC,* III, 833) He does not find this minimum of coparticipated political ideas in Spain, and there is also lacking a sense of justice.

This same lack of political conscience was evident in "the frustrated renovation or revolution of 1917," (*OC,* III, 837) which he calls a "general peaceful strike." There seemed to be a unanimity of desires without a unanimity of ideas, resulting in a frustrated prerevolutionary movement. The economic situation in Spain was grave with the majority of the nation suffering severe poverty, while in the great centers gold circulated freely. There were numerous political parties ranging from conservatives to extreme socialists. The lawyers were corrupt. The Spaniards lacked clear political ideas, and the initiative came from the Army. A new and unsuccessful government was formed, because the people basically acted with absolute lack of conscience and will.

This concludes the part of the volume on politics in the original edition (1918). In *OC,* III, and also in a recent volume, *Escritos políticos (Political Writings),*[4] a considerable number of articles have been added, written at later dates. The latter volume is more concise and contains some material not found in *OC,* III. Both cover later events, such as the dictatorship of Primo de Rivera (1923-1930), followed by the fall of the Monarchy, and the establishment of a Second Republic (1931). Pérez de Ayala had been opposed to the inefficiency of the Monarchy, and the tyranny of the Dictatorship, to which at one point he referred as the "senility of the Monarchy." Municipal elections were held in the spring of 1931, and the results made it clear that the King no longer had the support of his subjects. Without formally abdicating, he and his family departed for France.

In the fall of 1930, Pérez de Ayala and two other outstanding intellectuals, the well-known physician, Dr. Gregorio Marañón, and José Ortega y Gasset, distinguished professor of metaphysics at the University of Madrid, had formed a "League for the Defense of the Republic." There was strong support for their movement, despite the attempted intervention by the government. According to Ayala, during six days in February, there joined the movement some two or three thousand people per day, from many walks of life. (*EP*, p. 220)

The first public meeting was held in Segovia, and the words of Ayala's address were reported in *La Prensa* of Buenos Aires, since censorship in Spain made its appearance impossible in the Spanish press at that time. Referring to liberty, Ayala said that *authentic liberty consists not so much in the absence of external impediments, but rather in the total of favorable circumstances, so that each individual potentiality may fulfill its complete destiny and achieve its maximum social efficiency.* (*EP*, p. 225) He feels that their group has the role of affirming its right to be as they are, and that although they are called intellectuals, he is convinced that ideas are not out of place in political life.

In his opinion, "the modern State is a multiple and very delicate complex of creative potentialities in extreme tension. All for the State and the State for all, the potentiality of the individual for the State and of the State for the individual." (*EP*, p. 233) He finds ridiculous the theory that one must choose between monarchy and anarchy, which is in effect despotism or chaos. There must be a "just and harmonious balance," and this is the Republic.

Ayala deplores illiteracy as a national disgrace and believes that there should be equal opportunities for all, as well as equal justice. Equal education should include not only elementary but advanced education, or technical training, according to the aptitudes of the individual. These men of the League for the Republic had high ideals and did their best to form what they thought was right for Spain, a good Republic.

The various editions of *Política y toros* conclude with a discussion of bullfighting. Ayala declares that, although he is a devotee of bullfighting, if he were dictator of Spain, he would suppress the sport with a flourish of the pen. (*OC*, III, 810) Meanwhile, he attends bullfights because he finds them instructive and entertaining. They are a diversion that kills time, and time is the tyrant of man. They make him forget himself.

Although Ayala has lived in many countries, he finds their

people quite different from those Spaniards who form the public for bullfights. Their first characteristic is vain ignorance, and they do not, like other publics, recognize their deficiency. "The public in Spain wants to judge, which is typical of the intelligence which it lacks." (*OC*, III, 823) The public wants to be not only the judge but also the court. An Englishman attending a bullfight for the first time, reflecting on Spain's judgment remarked: "One might say that the spectators are the only people who know how to fight perfectly, and that the only ones who do not know how to fight are the bullfighters in the arena." (OC, III, 824)

The vain ignorance of the Spaniards is even more terrifying in the political field when they do not know that they themselves have formed Spain's political history, nor what this political history has been. Ayala concludes also that nowhere better than at a bullfight can one study the present psychology of the Spanish people. And just as life is a continual combat with death, the same is true of the bullfight.

V *Diplomatic Interim*

Following the organization of the Second Republic, headed during its first five years (1931-36) by Niceto Alcalá Zamora, various intellectuals were appointed to diplomatic posts, and Pérez de Ayala was named the Ambassador of Spain to Great Britain. Shortly before this appointment, he was also elected a Deputy of the Cortes and also Director of the Museum of the Prado. Some people have attributed these various appointments of the intellectuals to so many important posts as greed on their part, but in the opinion of others, it rather indicated a sufficient number of truly qualified men to fill these important posts.

Pérez de Ayala and his wife arrived in London in May 1931. We have not been able to find much evidence of his writing during his stay in London. It is probable that his diplomatic duties did not permit much time for literary activities. His widow has told us that he never accepted social invitations during the day, but he did go out in the evening. He was very popular, and numbered among his good friends the then Prince of Wales, now the Duke of Windsor.

When Einstein escaped from Germany and arrived in London, he spent two weeks at the Spanish Embassy as the friend of Pérez de Ayala. In Ayala's home in Madrid, there is a photograph dedicated to him by Einstein. Another friend in London at the time was Juan de La Cierva, inventor of the autogiro. The wife of Pérez de Ayala made a flight with the aviator in his new invention. Unamuno also visited Ayala when he went to England in 1936 to receive his *doctorado honoris causa* from the University of Oxford.

Ayala's life as an Ambassador was difficult because of the constant political unrest in Spain. After five years in London, he resigned his post in May, 1936, following the triumph of the leftist party, "El frente popular," in February, 1936. Before returning to Spain, Pérez de Ayala was made a *doctor honoris causa* by the University of London.

VI *Civil War and Post-Civil War Activities*

Pérez de Ayala returned to Madrid in July of 1936, the day after the assassination of Calvo Sotelo. In September of that year, he was obliged to leave Spain with the few possessions which he could carry, and learned later that his home and its contents had disappeared as if by magic. According to his widow, the family, aided by British officials, left Spain from Alicante on an English warship which took them to Marseilles. They went first to Biarritz to join their friends, the Marañóns, and later went to Paris, where they spent the period of the Spanish Civil War (1936-1939) together with many distinguished Spanish friends such as Azorín, Pío Baroja, and Sebastián Miranda. Pérez de Ayala continued writing articles and some poetry. He had to live by his pen, and perhaps for that reason he did not write novels whose publication would have been impossible at that time. His writings appeared in South American newspapers, and many of them are still uncollected, according to J. García Mercadal.

The two sons of Pérez de Ayala joined Franco's army during the Spanish Civil War, as did also the son of Ortega y Gasset. Ayala and his wife returned briefly after the War. A literary career in Spain at that time was very difficult. Invited to give lectures in various parts of South America, Ayala went with his wife to that continent in 1940, and he lectured in Peru and

Chile. The family finally became established in Buenos Aires, where Ayala wrote articles for *La Prensa* and found there many Spanish friends such as Ortega y Gasset and others.

The Ayala family returned to Spain to stay in the fall of 1954. K. W. Reinink is of the opinion that conditions in Buenos Aires influenced his decision, such as "the confiscation of *La Prensa* by the Perón regime," and a certain degree of suppression of the liberty of the press.[5] Ayala's widow told us that while all of this may have had some influence on his decision, the most compelling reason was the death of his elder son, Juan, leaving a wife and children in Spain. His other son, Eduardo, who had an influential position with the Shell Oil Company, also returned to Spain and became Chief of Personnel with Shell Oil in Madrid. Although he never recovered from his grief over the loss of his elder son, Pérez de Ayala was happy to be with his family in Spain until his death in August of 1962. He was a devoted husband, father, and grandfather.

VII *Essays Pertaining to Literature*

While Pérez de Ayala was occupied in his earlier days with his writings on war and politics, he was also busy writing essays pertaining to literary subjects and literary criticism. One of his important contributions was a two-volume edition of *Las máscaras* (1917-1919), now to be found also in *OC*, III (1963), together with a third part apparently added to *Las máscaras* for the first time. These essays are undated so that it is difficult to arrange them chronologically. The three parts of this work occupy some 650 pages of *OC*, III. Space permits only a rather summary discussion of the work which is largely dramatic criticism.

For the 1940 edition of *Las máscaras*, Ayala wrote a Prologue expressing repentance for some of his adverse criticism of the Spanish dramatist, Benavente, in this work, feeling that he uttered some of these opinions at an impetuous age whe he enjoyed polemics. He also wrote that he would not agree later with some of his theatrical theories set forth in the earlier edition.

The volume opens with a discussion of the Spanish novelist and dramatist Pérez Galdós, and a defense of him against critics who find him heavy and boring, especially in his drama. In a comparison of Cervantes and Galdós, Ayala states that "Cervantes created the novelistic type, this modern literary type characteristic of the Modern Age; Galdós has carried it in Spain to the greatest fulfillment of perfection and maturity." As to drama, Ayala feels that in an age, "much more depraved and corrupt than that of three centuries ago," Galdós has brought to the Spanish stage a simple and realistic theater. (*OC,* III, 47) Cervantes was not the leading dramatist of his age, but according to Ayala, Galdós is without dispute the leading dramatist in our age, and one of the first of any age or place. Always loyal to his great friend, Galdós, he remarks elsewhere that "Galdós has tragic depth and democratic substance" and compares him to the Greeks, Shakespeare, and Tolstoi, with "compassion" which is not Hellenic but Christian. (*OC,* III, 406) He also admires his great tolerance.

Ayala criticizes Benavente for his attacks on the editors of *España* at the same time that in his dramas he preaches brotherly love. But it is an intellectual type of love, which sounds false. He comments favorably on the elegance and versatility of Benavente's theater, but finds that the characters are more interesting for their external appearance than for their souls. He feels, too, that Benavente has tried to impose on the Spanish theater inferior categories from foreign sources. His theater is antitheatrical, without passion and without any true reality. He affirms that the value of Benavente's theater is a negative value with too many disconnected episodes. It is cerebral and not linked with life. It lacks originality and suffers an aridity of true feeling.

Pérez de Ayala was a great admirer of the theater of Valle-Inclán and feels that all of his writings have a theatrical atmosphere. He is particularly impressed by Valle-Inclán's dynamism and great talent for dialogue. Of course, all of this was written in 1917 and refers to the early theater of Valle-Inclán. Ayala would undoubtedly have been even more enthusiastic about the later theater of Valle-Inclán, such as *Divinas palabras* (1920) and his many *Esperpentos* that followed.

There is an interesting discussion of the various versions of the Don Juan theme, including that of Bernard Shaw, which he finds different in that it is based on aggressive ideas which inspire both emotions and polemics. He is convinced that Shaw considered his Don Juan from a philosophical standpoint. In summary, Ayala considers Don Juan both cosmopolitan and universal, stating that "The universal is everlasting while the cosmopolitan evolves in accord with changing times and customs." (*OC*, III, 386)

There are essays on less important dramatists in all three parts of *Las máscaras,* which we shall omit for consideration of space, and not for lack of interest. In writing of the theatrical crisis in Spain, Ayala remarks that people have been discussing the decadence or crisis of the theater since the days of Euripides and concludes: "As regards the Spanish theater, since the Golden Age we have not had so many nor such excellent dramatists as now." (*OC*, III, 555)

Although Pérez de Ayala had such a great knowledge and understanding of the theater, he has, as far as we can find out, written and had published only one play, brief and of minor importance, *Sentimental Club* (1909), now available as *La revolución sentimental,* in *OC,* II. It is a kind of burlesque satire on communism which seems to have suppressed a number of earthly amenities except love, and to have transformed things considerably. The group of the Sentimental Club propose to establish a Sentimental Revolution in which love will be the solution to their puzzling problems.

Among the essays of a literary nature is the collection in *Divagaciones literarias.* The book includes an article in memoriam to Rubén Darío, who died in 1916, and whom Ayala has always regarded as an "immortal man." Ayala affirms that "Rubén Darío is the most musical poet and the most poetic troubadour of all those who have sung in the Castilian language."[6] He admires Darío's gift of words and sound, and as for metrics: "It suffices to say that there is no meter of those used in the Castilian language, since its origins, which Rubén Darío does not know in its most secret mechanism and consequently uses with perfect grace and insuperable mastery." (P. 124)

There is also in this same volume a tribute to Zorrilla for the centenary of his birth. Since Zorrilla was born in 1817, it is to be assumed that the tribute was written in 1917, and in it he also refers to World War I. Not having read Zorrilla for some years, Ayala does not wish to repeat the many platitudes already written. He does not consider Zorrilla a great or inspired poet, but he had the gift of languages. "Zorilla brought poetry to its elemental source; the intrinsic value of the word. Something like what the French Impressionists did with painting, restoring to it the intrinsic value of light." (P. 64) He concludes that "Zorrilla was the live spirit of the language; a man graced with the insuperable gift of the word. Let us admire him and take from him the oral wealth which he left us, but let us avoid imitating him in the rest of his poetry. His poetry was unconscious grace, but not art. And grace is received, but not imitated. Nothing would be so unfortunate for a present-day poet as to imitate Zorrilla." (P. 65)

There is a long discussion of Juan Valera the man, and to some extent his work, written some time after Valera's death in 1926. One English critic declared that Juan Valera achieved the most elevated form of art by combining seriousness in depth with lightness in form, but Valera himself declared that his novelistic purpose was simply to entertain and distract. He wished, like the Greek Longus, to manipulate the emotions of his characters without becoming emotionally involved himself. Valera was often called a skeptic, but Ayala points out that this word from its Greek root "means to observe, examine, think and weigh and ponder over reality itself." (P. 95) In this sense, Valera was a skeptic. Ayala also declares that Valera was the most complete humanist and with the most natural mastery of ancient letters that he had ever known. In these aspects Valera and Ayala were much alike.

Valera's mother was a Marquesa and wanted a political career for her son, but he was unimpressed by professional politicians. In order to please her, however, he did allow himself to be elected deputy to the Cortes, but he disliked oratory. He served for some time in the diplomatic service. Although he spurned a political career, he was deeply concerned with politics and the welfare of his country, and within his novels, written supposedly "to distract and entertain," one can easily sense his social and political preoccupations. In this he was again like Ayala. Pérez de Ayala believed that Valera for his attitude toward literary art, falls within the classic age of Greek culture.

In the same volume, there are a number of pages devoted to Pérez Galdós in which Ayala gives further evidence of his admiration for his lifelong friend, remarking that the very mention of the formidable name of Galdós awakens in him a feeling of reverence, a reverence which is love. He feels that "religious emotion gravitates, like an atmosphere of Elysian light, over the work of Cervantes of yesteryear and the work of Galdós today." He defines religious emotion as a "sensation of presence (of death) and a feeling of reverence (toward the fundamental values of life)." (P. 139) Ayala feels that the great majority of the works of Galdós develop the religious problem as a problem supremely human.

In the opinion of Ayala, in the nineteenth century there are only two writers whose works are filled with a religious atmosphere. The writers are Galdós and "Clarín." He finds this same atmosphere evident in all of the writers of the later Generation of 1898, and he especially mentions Unamuno, Azorín, Maetzu, Grandmontagne, Valle-Inclán, and Baroja. We should question the works of Baroja as having much religious atmosphere, but Christian charity he has. The work of Valle-Inclán is also doubtful as characterized by a religious atmosphere. The activities of the Marqués de Bradomín are ironically irreverent, to say the least.

Finally, referring to Galdós as Don Benito, el Bueno, Ayala declares that Don Benito was incapable of speaking ill of anyone. He was constantly aiding the poor with the income from his writings, for he could conceive of no other real use for money. Writing further of Valle-Inclán, he says: "I see in the essence of all the work of Valle-Inclán a remote and sacred dramatization, a titanic and fierce sensation of the endless struggle between absolute Good and Evil," (p. 198) not as metaphysical concepts but live entities. He often finds in Valle-Inclán an aesthetic emotion at its peak, an emotion of ecstasy. Summing up the value of Valle-Inclán's work, Ayala comments: "It might be said that the work of Valle-Inclán takes form and moves in the spheres of the imagination, in a world of pure and necessary realities; and his person becomes incorporeal in the sphere of fantasy, of arbitrariness, as if the elemental laws of the physical world did not dominate this strange man in his daily life." (P. 195)

Included in this book are interesting commentaries on Azorín, probably written some time after 1924, the year of the great Alicantine's election to the Royal Spanish Academy, to which Ayala refers. His discussion of Azorín's novel *Doña Inés* reveals Ayala's keen critical genius. He appreciates Azorín's inimitable style, using the often-repeated phrase of Buffon: "The style is the man." Azorín's style is such that a literate reader could identify the author after reading a few sentences, whether it be the description of a landscape or an ancient ruin. Ayala finds in his works "Plasticity, incomparable fineness. Pictorial values and spiritual content. Stylistic wealth and sobriety, and at the same time classical influences." His early nihilism has now "developed toward an elegant Horatian skepticism." (P. 246) He is always moved by sympathy for the weak and oppressed, and seeks social justice.

These essays on Azorín are repeated in the volume *Ante Azorín (In the Presence of Azorín)*, 1964, and other essays on the great writer are undated. Ayala comments: "Personality is that which one carries with him everywhere. One of the most definite and genuinely literary personalities in contemporary Spanish literature is that of Azorín."[7] Ayala feels that "the prose of Azorín is the most expressive and evident integral part of his personality. Before him no one wrote as he in Castilian. Nor after him does anyone resemble him; and those who resemble him least are those who try to imitate him." (P. 139) Ayala feels that Azorín's literary criticism has absolute originality because of his distinct personality. He knows how to collaborate with the subject of his criticism, be it a writer or painter. He has been an orator in the Cortes, and a tireless traveler who has painted Castile with an art that reveals at the same time the soul of the landscape and the soul of Azorín. He is himself in his numerous short stories, novels, essays, and dramas.

Azorín's work is filled with an aesthetic dynamism. Time as an objective reality is his great preoccupation, and "he tends always to perpetuate the present" (p. 151) to escape the painful and tragic sensation of the transitory aspect of time. There seems to be a duality in Azorín, who senses time as a permanent and uninterrupted present, but on the other hand, he has "the noble and sad gesture of an exile from eternity which he feels and longs for as his native land." (P. 160)

Ayala is especially interested in Azorín's play *Angelita* (1930), and the sensation of time so originally incorporated therein. He is also interested in his novels *Felix Vargas* (1928), now entitled *El caballero inactual*, and in *Superrealismo* (1929), now entitled *El libro de Levante*. These works were written in what has frequently been called Azorín's "surrealistic" period, stupidly so called, in the opinion of Ayala. It has also been called *van-*

guardista. Ayala considers these two novels and some of his theater to be the most Azorinian of his works, and remarks that Azorín was always a *vanguardista* and revolutionary in his ingenuous personality." (P. 142)

We should say that Azorín's tendencies were always in the direction of the vanguard since his earliest writings, but essentially Azorinian. As Ayala says, no great writer can be anything but himself. That Azorín was a youthful rebel in *La voluntad* is undoubtedly true, but his rebellion has changed toward more mature directions as the years have passed. We agree with the author of *Ante Azorín* that these works mentioned do mark a high point in Azorín's career.

Pointing out the qualities that distinguish and define the works of Azorín, Ayala finds them to be "subtlety, smoothness, ingenuity, and humor." They possess an "exquisite subtlety," a kind of weightlessness, and they have a "spontaneous polish." (P. 178) After some discussion of humor, both misguided and genuine, Ayala concludes that Azorín "is an authentic humorist. In him we find all the ingredients of humor, in the proper proportion: irony, satire, wit (the two latter with a delicate and elegant tone), an intellectual transcendency and a subjective transcendency (human sympathy)." (P. 222) In our opinion, Azorín's humor is always subtle and kindly. The only thing that Azorín lacks, according to Ayala, is "the creation of great ideal figures." We feel that was not Azorín's goal. He was interested in the little man who might, in his own small way, be a "great and ideal figure." Azorín wanted to create a "great and ideal" Spain.

Más divagaciones literarias, 1960 is more or less a companion volume to *Divagaciones literarias,* and fortunately its articles are identified as to time and source, with dates ranging from 1922 to 1959. The volume opens with a scholarly discussion of the concept of style, containing references to noted authors, both classic and more contemporary. One of Ayala's conclusions refers to the style of Cervantes as "the expression of a spiritual elegance, sad, indolent, tolerant, and smiling. And this hidden elegance one possesses or does not possess; but it is not acquired, nor forced, nor imitated." (P. 19)

We have already mentioned Ayala's rather extensive study of Nietzsche. There is a tribute to Anatole France on the occasion of his death (1924). As further evidence of his wide interest in foreign literatures, we find a brief study of a novel of Turgenef, and a much longer discussion of the Portuguese writer, Eça de Queiroz.

One of the relatively recent essays is "Humanidades" ("Humanities,") 1959, in which the author discourses on one of his favorite subjects. He feels that "The Humanities" are "the substance of culture," and that the "classics contain the most intense saturation of Humanism and of humanity; or in other words human experience." ((P. 231) He foresees a rebirth and a new interpretation of the classic spirit as contemporaneous.

Ayala is convinced that some people find the classics boring because they are an acquired taste, but acquired tastes are the most satisfactory and also the most difficult to renounce, just as the tastes for alcohol and tobacco. But the difference lies in the fact that "those relative and artificial paradises of Bacchus and tobacco impose on us considerable physiological and economic servitude," while "habitual contact and intimacy with the classics transports us to an authentic delight of the full consciousness of life; . . . they bring us a kind of Edenic forgetfulness and serene elevation, at the same time that they restore our health and vigor of spirit." (P. 261)

Later Ayala observes that man, by reading good books, can conquer time and space: "When man has a good book in his hand, his personality suddenly prolongs itself through all of space and the whole extent of time both past and future. And he even achieves union with God: an intuition of eternity in a single instant of creation. Then can it truly be said that man is the king of creation." (Pp. 302-3)

The author's love of the classics is also reflected in *Fábulas y ciudades (Fables and Cities)*, 1961, with essays dating from 1948 to 1957. In the first half of the book, he comments with his usual originality on the fables and myths of the past. He finds more truth in fable than in life and remarks: "Life is the great teacher; the fable is its amanuensis."[8] But one must live first to understand the truth of the fable.

The second half of the book is dedicated to essays on the great cities of antiquity, such as Alexandria, which he calls "the golden wedding ring between East and West." (P. 120) He feels that "Athens is the mother of wisdom and knowledge." (P.

124) Ayala pays tribute to Rome with its ancient temples and fabulous past, and also to the great philosophers, such as Plato and Aristotle.

In the essays of Ayala, collected up to the present, we have found relatively little reference to the Spanish Civil War and its aftermath, nor to the Second World War, but they were years of suffering for him, as evidenced by what he wrote about 1940 or 1941, regarding his favorite reading. Ayala found permanent comfort in reading Job, the *Consolation* of the Roman philosopher, Boethius, *The Imitation of Christ* by Thomas a Kempis, the *Memorial of Santa Helena,* and the fables of Aesop and Phaedrus. He explains that the first three are "twilight works in whose waning light life lengthens its shadow on one side, while from the other side it receives splendors *sub specie aeterni,* like glimpses of the immortal." Aesop and Phaedrus, on the other hand, seem to bring a kind of "morning dawn of human reason." (P. 10)

Job and Kempis continue to be his frequent reading and he has translated some of their chapters. He has also translated into verse some of the fables of Phaedrus. His great interest in Job and Kempis further supports our belief in his sincere religious faith.

We have already mentioned *Principios y finales de la novela* (1958), which, aside from some already quoted commentaries on the general nature of the novel, contains a number of critical essays, largely on English and other foreign authors, which we shall omit because they seem less important than some of his other essays. *Amistades y recuerdos* (1961), also already mentioned, contains essays regarding his own friendships and recollections, many of them essays of rather recent date. He is, as always, a faithful admirer of "Clarín," the master of his youth, as well as of his other masters, Valera and Menéndez Pelayo. He points out that Leopoldo Alas was a professor known only to his students, while as "Clarín," (name of a character of Calderón's *La vida es sueño*), his words as a writer were known to the world. Because he was a great teacher, he was a great writer. Ayala remarks: "The educative function is not so much teaching (providing an inorganic mass of data and knowledge) as formation and development of the spirit . . ." (P. 17) This "formation and development of the spirit," Leopoldo Alas achieved.

Also Ayala writes: "For a profoundly religious spirit, the aristocrat of the intelligence must be a man of faith." (P. 20)

In the second half of the nineteenth century, there are, according to Ayala, "seven great Spanish novelists, Valera, Alarcón, Galdós, Pereda, Pardo Bazán, "Clarín," and Palacio Valdés." (P. 31) Most of them had resolved their economic problems before beginning to write. None of them could live from his literary profits except Galdós, who, because of his extreme generosity in charity was no better off financially than the others. Their writing was a spiritual luxury. Ayala calls Pardo Bazán "a Lope with skirts, a monster (prodigy) of Nature." (P. 55) She had a great capacity and wrote every type of literature, but she excelled in the narrative.

Ayala also pays tribute to the great sculptor, Julio Antonio, and the great painters José Rodríguez Acosta and Darío de Regoyos. He writes of Granada with true artistic appreciation, and also of some of her sculptors who worked in polychrome. The volume is filled with personal impressions of a whole gallery of illustrious figures in the world and the literature of the nineteenth and twentieth centuries, impressions too numerous to mention. The book is written in a delightfully human style and expresses keenly perceptive judgments.

In 1963 appeared the volume *Pequeños ensayos,* consisting of some one hundred essays, collected by J. García Mercadal. These "Little Essays" originally came out in various Spanish newspapers and were largely written in an earlier period of Ayala's career, between 1909 and 1928. They cover a wide diversity of subjects, war, literature, writers such as Alarcón, "Clarín," Pereda, and once more Ayala's beloved Galdós. He considers that masculine sensitivity is greater than feminine, but that in this matter "Pardo Bazán approaches, as far as it is possible for a woman, creative masculinity." (P. 308)

The recently published essays of *Nuestro Séneca (Our Seneca),* 1966, have, as the title suggests, a number of pages devoted to the Spanish-born Roman-educated philosopher. Ayala agrees with the affirmation of Angel Ganivet that the Senecan philosophy, largely Stoic, has greatly influenced the Spanish psychology. The name of Seneca and references to his ideas appear frequently in Spanish literature. Ayala judges him first among the Spanish

Latin writers of the beginning of the Christian era because he is "the most Spanish and the most universal."[9] Ayala considers him as a man and as a writer. In his smile on his statue there is a bit of irony which seems to transform itself into a "compassionate, thoughtful melancholy," and "comprehensive tolerance." (P. 26) As a youth, Seneca was gifted with an elegant power of speech, oratory, and style. He believed in "the absolute truth, which is nothing but the highest good: God." Ayala quotes a maxim from Seneca: "No one is truly honorable without believing in God." (P. 45)

There exist nine authentic tragedies of Seneca with Greek subjects, largely from Euripides. It is commonly said that "Euripides innovated the Greek tragedy, introducing psychological analysis and observation of the soul of the human character." (P. 49) Ayala feels that "Seneca, for his part, goes farther and more deeply and extensively into his psychological penetration." He introduced scenic art. And with his overflowing humanity "he sought in each Roman, the man." (P. 51) He was intensely modern and, with his profound humanity, "he sought to put side by side the love of pure science and the duty of carrying out something useful and convenient for others."

Among other essays in the volume is "Espejo de desterrados" ("A Mirror of the Exiled"), in which Ayala seeks perhaps to make some restitution for his attacks on the Jesuits, especially in A. M. D. G. He tells of the expulsion of the Jesuits from Spain by Carlos II, in 1767, follows the vicissitudes of their flight, and writes of several Jesuit abbots in the group who, in Ayala's words, were "for Jesuits, extremely cultured people" (p. 144) and fervent defenders of their native Spain, wherever they went.

Four of them "produced during their stay in Italy, several monumental works which initiate, and on the highest level, four of the most outstanding disciplines in the culture of our days. The abbot Hervás y Panduro creates comparative linguistics, and, up to a certain point, anthropology. The abbot Andrés is the first to trace a complete panorama of general comparative literature." (P. 147) The abbot Arteaga wrote a treatise on aesthetics. The abbot Masdeu was a forerunner in "conceiving a critical history, in which history is viewed not as a successive chronology of courtly events, but as an evolutionary development of a civilization and a culture." (P. 147)

There was also an abbot Lampillo who was among the first to study Latin literature in depth with special attention to the great Hispanic writers. Thus Pérez de Ayala has finally paid tribute to some of the Jesuits. It would be interesting to know when these essays were written, but all the essays in the book are undated, except the final one written in memory of Rubén Darío in 1916.

VIII *Evaluation*

It is difficult to formulate an adequate evaluation of Ayala's nonfictional prose in this necessarily selective choice from his essays, very brief in proportion to the hundreds of his essays available in book form. We can only say that they form a very important part of his literary achievement, and it is hoped that J. García Mercadal will continue his valuable efforts in collecting and editing the essays of Pérez de Ayala. Many of them are of great literary value, and they also shed much light on the personality, the profound and varied ideas, and the vast knowledge of their author.

CHAPTER 7

Conclusion

P EREZ DE AYALA has written that a work of art must give a
sensation of life. Life in all its infinite variety and unlimited
problems is vividly portrayed in his own writings. As we review
his works, we see the development of his spirit. From his
earliest juvenile efforts, it is evident that he was born to write,
and enthusiasm and love of creation are constantly evident in
his work. In his earliest volume of poetry, the tone is more
personal and youthful, often times emotional, as he seeks peace
and finds God in the beauties of Nature. Then he abandons
poetry temporarily and begins his novelistic career.

His four important early novels have their autobiographical
element in the theme of the anguished experiences of the developing artist and writer. The structure is somewhat episodic
with a large number of characters, essential to Ayala's firm
belief that man can understand life and its problems only by
viewing it from many perspectives. His personal attitude is to
observe but not to judge. Important, too, in these novels is the
author's preoccupation for the ills of Spain, reflecting similar
preoccupations in the writings of the Generation of 1898. Ayala
is concerned at this period not only for Spain, but also for
Europe, for their current cultural, social, and political problems,
and their future.

We recall that his first volume of poems, highly praised by
Rubén Darío, bears at its beginning a reference to Edgar Allan
Poe's "struggle to apprehend the supernal Loveliness." Pérez
de Ayala has been successful in this struggle in most of his poetry,
to which he returns after his early novels. His later poems to
the sea and to the river reveal more of a philosophical trend
together with what has been called an "intellectual emotion." He
portrays the dynamic beauty and the infinite variations of the

sea, symbolic also of the endless variations of man, and his philosophical trend frequently ends a poem with a didactic note. In these poems his gift for language is marked by great lyricism and is frequently lightened by humor, at times burlesque. He handles with the skill of a true poet the metrical variations suitable to the themes, often very original in their combinations. The poem which closes the volume to the river, "Philosophy," (*OC*, II, 205-8), in the opinion of many critics, is the expression of the author's ideal, as he seeks harmony between man and the universe.

His three *Poematic Novels of Spanish Life* are what the title implies. They continue a portrayal of man's philosophical and personal problems and strong criticism of the deficiencies of Spain. Each chapter is headed by a charming poem expressing in lyric essence what may be expected within the chapter in prose. In poetic style, careful construction, and psychological penetration, they far excel the first four novels, although there still continue the major notes of pessimism and tragedy. In these novels man does not manage to solve his problems, but he does make an effort.

In his last three major novels, two of them bipartite, Pérez de Ayala reached the height of his novelistic career. He abandoned his early somewhat autobiographical themes and now creates strong, often symbolic characters. There is, however, a new note of optimism as man meets and solves his problems. Belarmino, fascinated by words, seeks to create for himself a new and hermetic vocabulary, thus reflecting the author's great linguistic interests. Belarmino becomes more and more an introvert, but he is intensely human in his devotion to his adopted daughter. Apolonio, the philosopher-dramatist, is an extrovert who seeks glory. The two shoemakers are two sides of a single personality, eventually achieving mutual comprehension and harmony in their final reunion and fraternal embrace. Urbano and Simona emerge from their Edenic innocence and through their own efforts achieve a meaningful marriage. The great and responsible Tigre Juan finds within himself the strength to reject the old traditional code of honor and through his love becomes a happy husband and father. In each of these novels, Pérez de Ayala has achieved a part of universal harmony which was his goal.

Ayala's great preoccupation with the world in crisis and his

own personal problems cause him to abandon his fictional career for journalistic writing, which he considers more familiar
and subjective. He can speak to his readers directly and per-
sonally, not through a fictional character. As he once said, he
can reveal himself as a man and also as "a mirror of the universe." In his hundreds of essays on an infinite variety of subjects, he has done just that. His essays reveal him as human,
comprehensive, and erudite, as he writes of classical subjects,
current problems, great literary figures, and his many illustrious
friends.

Throughout his works we find what he considers the "eternal
norms": love in many variations; and devotion to his native soil,
Asturias, which is the setting in practically all of his novels, but
the novels are not regional. The characters, from all walks of
life, are individuals that are not only Asturians, but universal
in their emotions, in the problems which they confront and resolve. They are types that have existed in world literature and
life for cenutries: rogues, rascals, prostitutes, peasants, common
people, nobility, with all their weaknesses and strength. The
author's descriptions of some of the nobility are especially humorous and ironic, but not cruel. Ayala has given his characters
individuality and treated them with comprehension and tolerance.

Pérez de Ayala has never forgotten what he considers to be
the "vital values": religion, ethics, and aesthetics. As for ethics,
Ayala has revealed in all his work a basically high standard of
moral values and fair-dealing in man's relationship to man.
While in his early novels there are characters with low moral
standards comparable to those of the picaresque tradition, the
author makes it clear that such a code of living does not pay.
At the same time, he has understanding and compassion for
man's weaknesses. In his later novels, he portrays characters of
great moral strength and integrity, such as Tigre Juan. His
writings are not unduly didactic.

Ayala's works have a pronounced philosophical vein as he is
ever in search of Truth, Beauty, and Good, both in man and
nature, but his writings are interspersed with humor and irony
which relieve them of excessive erudition. He is basically a poet
in verse or prose and can even find poetic values in such unlikely
things as the printing press. His descriptions of Nature reveal
his artistic perception of line and color and all the sensory

aspects of natural beauty, and also his talent to paint them. His tremendous wealth of vocabulary reflects his great intellectual interests and his ardent reading of the classics. His breadth of viewpoint is evident in his constant use of varied perspectives and contrasts. He believes that nothing is all bad or all good, except for God who is the Supreme Good.

From the mention in his early poem, "The Peaceful Path," of finding God in the peace of Nature, which some will construe as pantheistic, we find in his works constant serious references to God and to religion. His early interest in religion is expressed in an essay dated 1907, and found in *Tribute to England*. He writes that religion "is an insatiable thirst for purity and an ideal." Forgetting himself, man gives himself freely "with infinite love to all beings and all things." Religion is further "strength in adversity and simplicity in daily life, it is an oil spread over existence which makes us slip toward death, without bitterness and without horror." (P. 195) There is no indication that Pérez de Ayala has ever changed these ideas of his regarding religion. These ideals are manifest in his life and works. Further evidence of his religious interest is found in the choice of his favorite readings: Job, Kempis, and the Bible.

Various critics have commented that Pérez de Ayala is not a "popular" writer because of his excessive erudition. It is unlikely that he would want to write popular works, usually read by a public interested in plot and action, not in character study and psychological motivations, aesthetic beauty, or philosophical speculations. It is significant that Ayala has been highly praised by the great literary figures of his time, such as Rubén Darío, Pérez Galdós, Ortega y Gasset, and other eminent writers. Nor has the literary world of today forgotten him. Articles are frequently published in scholarly magazines on various aspects of his writings. A number of doctoral dissertations have been written on his works. It is interesting, too, that some of his novels have been translated and published in countries as far apart as Germany and Japan.

Pérez de Ayala has been honored in Spain and abroad. In 1926, he was awarded the Spanish National Prize for Literature for one of his major novels. In the same year, he was elected to the Royal Spanish Academy but remained member-elect until his death, as he never seemed to find a propitious time to make the entrance address necessary for formal reception into the Academy. The University of London awarded him an honorary Doctor's degree in 1936. In New York, in 1949, the Hispanic Society in the United States awarded him their medal, at the same time similarly honoring several other distinguished Spaniards, such as Juan Ramón Jiménez and José Ortega y Gasset. In 1960, he won the important Spanish Juan March Prize for creative literature.

The universal appeal of Pérez de Ayala's writings is evidenced in the unique and lyric beauty of his poetry with its originality of meter, its symbolism, and its philosophical implications; in his major novels in which he creates strong characters whose problems are those of mankind; and in his essays which cover a world of thought and interpretation of subjects pertaining to almost every aspect of the universe. His works are characterized by a beauty and richness of style which few can equal.

Notes and References

Chapter One

1. *Amistades y recuerdos* (Barcelona, 1961), p. 300. Hereafter cited as *Amistades*.
2. *El país del futuro* (Madrid, 1959), p. 24. Hereafter cited as *País*.
3. José Ortega y Gasset, *Meditaciones del Quijote* (Buenos Aires, 1942). See pp. 13-45.
4. See this essay (1903), in *Rincón asturiano*, a collection of essays dating from 1903 to 1925, now found only in Pérez de Ayala's *Obras completas*, Vol. I. See especially pp. 1085-87. The three present volumes of these *Obras completas* (Madrid 1964, 1965, 1966) will henceforth have references from them cited in the text as *OC*, with appropriate volume and page included.
5. It is strange that so many otherwise reliable critics and reputable publishers have recently been giving the year of Pérez de Ayala's birth as 1881, which is incorrect. His early critic and biographer, F. Agustín, gives 1880 as his birth date, as does also J. García Mercadal, who has spent so many years on the study of Pérez de Ayala. We saw the great Asturian's baptismal certificate in his home in Madrid. This certificate clearly gives his birth date as August 9, 1880.
6. Francisco Agustín, *Ramón Pérez de Ayala—Su vida y obras* (Madrid, 1927), pp. 15, 16. Hereafter cited as Agustín.
7. Julio Trenas, "Visita a Ramón Pérez de Ayala," *Indice* (Madrid, Sept.-Oct., 1958), p. 5. Hereafter referred to as Trenas.
8. *Ante Azorín* (Madrid, 1964), pp. 11, 12.
9. *Tributo a Inglaterra* (Madrid, 1963), p. 317. Hereafter cited as *Tributo*.
10. Santiago Riopérez y Milá, "Ramón Pérez de Ayala, otra vez poeta," *(ABC*, ed. aérea, April 16, 1959).
11. Graciela Palau de Nemes, *Vida y obra de Juan Ramón Jiménez* (Madrid, 1957), p. 90.

159

Chapter Two

1. Salvador de Madariaga, *The Genius of Spain and other essays on Spanish Contemporary Literature* (London, 1930), p. 79. Hereafter cited as Madariaga.

2. Angel Valbuena Prat, *Historia de la literatura española* (Barcelona, 1950), III, 518. Hereafter cited as Valbuena.

3. Titus Carus Lucretius, *De rerum natura,* English translation by H. A. J. Munro (London, 1864).

4. Juan-Eduardo Cirlot, *Diccionario de símbolos tradicionales* (Barcelona, 1958), p. 379.

5. César Barja, *Libros y autores contemporáneos* (New York, 1935), p. 457. Hereafter cited as Barja.

Chapter Three

1. *Principios y finales de la novela* (Madrid, 1958), p. 10. Hereafter cited as *Novela.*

2. *Pequeños ensayos* (Madrid, 1963), p. 31.

3. Prologue by author for Argentine edition of *Troteras y danzaderas* (Buenos Aires, 1942), pp. 5-21. Hereafter cited as Prologue. In our study, the text of the novel itself will be cited from *OC,* I.

4. "Cartas inéditas de Pérez de Ayala a Galdós," edited by José Schraibman. *Hispanófila,* 17 (Madrid, 1963), pp. 88-89. Hereafter cited as "Cartas."

5. *Tinieblas en las cumbres,* 3d ed. (Madrid, 1928).

6. *A. M. D. G.* (Madrid: Renacimiento, 1911). This edition used for our study.

7. José Ortega y Gasset, *Obras completas,* 2d ed. (Madrid, 1950), I, 532-35.

8. Norma Urrutia, *De Troteras a Tigre Juan.* Madrid: Insula, 1960, p. 41.

9. See unsigned Introduction to *Selections from Pérez de Ayala,* edited by Nicholson B. Adams and Sterling A. Stoudemire (New York, 1945), p. xii.

10. *Divagaciones literarias* (Madrid, 1958), pp. 291-92. Hereafter referred to as *Divagaciones.*

11. See article by Donald Fabian, "The Progress of the Artist: A Major Theme in the Early Novels of Pérez de Ayala," *(Hispanic Review,* XXVI, [1958], especially p. 14.

Chapter Four

1. These three *novelas poemáticas* and *El ombligo del mundo* are now published in Ayala's *Obras completas,* II (Madrid, 1965), and we shall refer to them from this edition.

2. Gonzalo Sobejano, *Nietzsche en España* (Madrid, 1967), p. 595.

3. *Más divagaciones literarias* (Madrid, 1960), pp. 65-130. Hereafter referred to as *Más divagaciones*.

Chapter Five

1. *Belarmino y Apolonio* (Buenos Aires, 1944). This edition used in our study.

2. *Luna de miel, luna de hiel* (Buenos Aires, 1958). This third edition used in our study.

3. *Los trabajos de Urbano y Simona* (Buenos Aires, 1962). This third edition used in our study.

4. *Tigre Juan*, in *Obras selectas de Pérez de Ayala* (Barcelona, 1957). This edition is used in our study. *Obras selectas* will henceforth be cited as *OS* in our text.

5. *El curandero de su honra*, in *Obras selectas* of Ayala. This edition will be cited in our text.

6. Frances Wyers Weber, *The Literary Perspectivism of Ramón Pérez de Ayala* (U. of North Carolina Press, 1966), p. 66.

7. Carlos Clavería, "Apostillas al lenguaje de Belarmino," in *Cinco estudios de literatura española moderna* (Salamanca, 1945), pp. 69-92.

8. Bernard Levy, "Pérez de Ayala's *Belarmino y Apolonio*," *Spanish Review*, III (New York, 1936), pp. 74-81.

9. Mary Ann Beck, "La realidad artística en las tragedias grotescas de Ramón Pérez de Ayala," *Hispania*, XLVI (New York, 1963), especially p. 483.

10. Jean Cassou, *Panorama de la Littérature Espagnole* (Paris, 1929), p. 131.

11. Leon Livingstone, "Interior Duplication and the Problem of Form in the Modern Spanish Novel," *PMLA*, LXXII (Sept. 1958), pp. 394-95.

12. Published by French and European Publications, 610 Fifth Avenue, New York, N. Y. 10020.

13. Mariano Baquero Goyanes, *Perspectivismo y contraste* (Madrid, 1963), p. 172.

14. José A. Balseiro, "Ramón Pérez de Ayala," *El vigía* (Madrid, 1928), II, 213-14.

15. See "Translator's Note" at the close of Walter Starkie's translation to English of *Tigre Juan* (New York, 1933), pp. 300-302.

16. Leon Livingstone, in article cited above in Note 11. See p. 405 of same article.

Chapter Six

1. *Hermann, encadenado* (Madrid, 1917).

2. *Obras selectas* (Barcelona, 1957), pp. 979-1167.
3. *Tabla rasa* (Madrid, 1963), p. 170.
4. *Escritos políticos* (Madrid, 1967). Hereafter cited as *EP*.
5. K. W. Reinink, *Algunos aspectos literarios y lingüísticos de la obra de Don Ramón Pérez de Ayala* (Utrecht, Holland, 1959), p. 45.
6. *Divagaciones literarias* (Madrid; Biblioteca Nueva, 1958), p. 114.
7. *Ante Azorín* (Madrid, 1964), p. 138.
8. *Fábulas y ciudades* (Barcelona, 1961), p. 11.
9. *Nuestro Séneca* (Barcelona, 1966).

Selected Bibliography

PRIMARY SOURCES

1. *Books by Pérez de Ayala*
(A few minor works omitted)
La paz del sendero (Madrid: Fernando Fe, 1903). Poetry.
Tinieblas en las cumbres (Madrid: Fernando Fe, 1907). Novel.
Sentimental Club (Madrid: Tip. Blass, 1909). Title later changed to *La revolución sentimental.* Short drama.
Sonreía (Madrid: Tip. Blas, 1909). Short novel.
A. M. D. G. (Madrid: Imprenta Artística Española, 1910). Novel of life in a Jesuit school.
La pata de la raposa (Madrid: Biblioteca Renacimiento, 1912). Novel.
La araña (Madrid: G. López del Horno, 1913). Short stories.
Troteras y danzaderas (Madrid: Biblioteca Renacimiento, 1913). Novel.
Prometeo, Luz de domingo, La caída de los Limones (Madrid: Imprenta Clásica Española, 1916). Three short poematic novels.
El sendero innumerable (Madrid: Imprenta Clásica Española, 1916). Poetry.
Hermann, encadenado (Madrid: Imprenta Clásica Española, 1917). Essays on visit to Italian front in World War I.
Las Máscaras, 2 vols. (Madrid: Renacimiento, 1917, 1919). Theatrical criticism.
Política y toros (Madrid: Calleja, 1918). Essays.
El sendero andante (Madrid: Jiménez y Molina, 1921). Also (Madrid: Calleja, 1921). Poetry.
Belarmino y Apolonio (Madrid: Calleja, 1921). Novel.
Luna de miel, luna de hiel (Madrid: Mundo Latino, 1923). Novel.
Los trabajos de Urbano y Simona (Madrid: Mundo Latino, 1923). Novel. (Continuation of preceding novel.)
El ombligo del mundo (Madrid: Rivadeneyra, Renacimiento, 1924). Five poematic novels with Prologue.

Bajo el signo de Artemisa (Madrid: Renacimiento, 1924). Short novels.

Tigre Juan (Madrid: Pueyo, 1926). Novel.

El curandero de su honra (Madrid: Pueyo, 1926). Novel (Continuation of *Tigre Juan.)*

Justicia (Madrid: Ed. unknown, 1928). Short novel.

El libro de Ruth (Madrid: Rivadeneyra, Paez, 1928). Anthology of essays taken from Ayala's novels.

Ramoneo (London: Concha Méndez y Manuel Altolaguirre, Impresores, 1935). Rare book; limited edition containing two new poems and the poetic prologues from Ayala's poematic novels.

Obras selectas (Barcelona: Ed. AHR, 1957). Novels and essays with Prologue by Nestor Luján.

Principios y finales de la novela (Madrid: Taurus, 1958). Essays.

Divagaciones literarias (Madrid: Biblioteca Nueva, 1958). Essays.

El país del futuro. Mis viajes a los Estados Unidos, 1913-1914; 1919-1920 (Madrid: Biblioteca Nueva, 1959). Essays.

Más divagaciones literarias (Madrid: Biblioteca Nueva, 1960). Essays.

Amistades y recuerdos (Barcelona: Aedos, 1961). Essays.

Fábulas y ciudades (Barcelona: Destino, 1961). Essays.

El Raposín (Madrid: Taurus, 1962). Short stories.

Tabla rasa (Madrid: Editorial Bullón, 1963). Essays.

Pequeños ensayos (Madrid: Biblioteca Nueva, 1963). Essays.

Tributo a Inglaterra (Madrid: Aguilar, 1963). Essays.

Ante Azorín (Madrid: Biblioteca Nueva, 1964). Essays.

Obras completas (not yet complete), 4 vols. (Madrid: Aguilar, 1964, 1965, 1966, 1969).

Nuestro Séneca y otros ensayos (Barcelona: E. D. H. A. S. A., 1966). Essays.

Escritos políticos (Madrid: Alianza Editorial, 1967). Essays.

English Translations

Prometheus. The Fall of the House of Limón. Sunday Sunlight. Short poetic novels of Spanish life. Prose translations by Alice P. Hubbard; poems by Grace Hazard Conkling (New York: E. P. Dutton and Co., 1920).

The Fox's Paw. Translation by Thomas Walsh (New York: E. P. Dutton and Co., 1924).

"Don Guillén and La Pinta": (first chapter of *Belarmino y Apolonio*), in *The European Caravan* (New York: Warren and Putnam, 1931).

"The Assistant Professor" (Title inexact. Ayala explains clearly in text of this story from *El ombligo del mundo* that the protagonist here is a substitute professor). Translated by Warre-Bradley

Wells. In *Great Spanish Short Stories* (Boston and New York: Houghton Mifflin Co., 1932.

Tiger Juan. Includes both parts of this bipartite novel, with good "Translator's Note." Translated by Walter Starkie, Litt. D. (New York: Macmillan, 1933). Also, British edition (London: Jonathan Cape, 1933).

SECONDARY SOURCES

ADAMS, N. B. and STOUDEMIRE, S. A. *Selections from Pérez de Ayala* (New York: Henry Holt, 1945). Contains very good discussion of the works of Pérez de Ayala in unsigned Introduction, pp. ix-xxxv.

AGUSTÍN, FRANCISCO. *Ramón Pérez de Ayala, su vida y obras* (Madrid: G. Hernández y Galo Sáez, 1927). Most complete interpretation of life and works of Ayala to 1927. Quite complimentary.

BALSEIRO, JOSÉ A. "Ramón Pérez de Ayala," *El Vigía, ensayos* (Madrid: Mundo Latino, 1928, II, 123-269). Very good analysis of the novels of Pérez de Ayala.

BAQUERO GOYANES, MARIANO. *Perspectivismo y contraste (de Cadalso a Pérez de Ayala)*. (Madrid: Gredos, 1963, pp. 160-244). Good study of Ayala's excellent use of perspective and contrast and other aspects of his work, such as the similarity between Ayala and Ortega in their concept of the novel as a tragicomedy.

BARJA, CÉSAR. *Libros y autores contemporáneos* (New York: Stechert, 1935). Excellent study of Pérez de Ayala, pp. 439-66.

BATAILLON, MARCEL. "Belarmino y Apolonio," *Bulletin Hispanique*, XXIV (1922), 189-91. Praises Ayala for his creation of live characters with significant problems, and for his wealth of vocabulary, ingenuity, fantasy, and humor.

BEARDSLEY, W. A. "Ayala's Latest: *Tigre Juan* and *Curandero de su honra*," *The Saturday Review of Literature*, May 15, 1926. Good review of this two-part novel in which the reviewer appreciates Ayala's non-melodramatic portrayal of love; his modern treatment of the code of honor; his stress on the importance of thought and self-understanding; and his creation of the character of Tigre Juan. He finds the verse in the novel excellent.

BECK, MARY ANN. "La realidad artística en las tragedias grotescas de Ramón Pérez de Ayala," *Hispania*, XLVI (1963), 480-89. Appreciates artistry of Ayala's major novels but fails to see the philosophy in *Belarmino y Apolonio*.

CARAYON, MARCEL. *Lumière des dimanches*, in *La Revue de Genève*, VI (1923). This French translation of *Sunday Sunlight* has Prologue by translator Carayon, discussing Ayala's early novels and his humanitarian sympathy for the unfortunate.

CASSOU, JEAN. "Ramón Pérez de Ayala," *Panorama de la Littérature Espagnole Contemporaine* (Paris: Kra, 1929), pp. 128-34. Cassou praises Ayala's extraordinary art in writing, condemns *A. M. D. G.*, and considers *Belarmino y Apolonio*, after *Don Quijote*, one of the greatest Spanish books.

CLAVERÍA, CARLOS. "Apostillas al lenguaje de Belarmino," *Cinco estudios de literatura española moderna* (Salamanca: C. S. I. C., 1945), pp. 69-91. Very interesting linguistic study, especially valuable to those interested in that subject.

_____. "Apostillas adicionales a *Belarmino y Apolonio*," *Hispanic Review* XVI (1948), 97-119. Further good study of Belarmino's language.

CURTIS, ERNEST ROBERT. "Ramón Pérez de Ayala," *Ensayos críticos acerca de la literatura europea*, 2 vols. (Barcelona: Seix Barral, 1959), II, 109-21. Meaningful discussion of philosophical and ethical questions in the novels of Pérez de Ayala.

FABIAN, DONALD L. "Action and Idea in *Amor y pedagogía* and *Prometeo*," *Hispania*, XLI (1958), interesting comparison of these two novels.

_____. "Pérez de Ayala and the Generation of 1898," *Hispania*, XLI, (1958). Title self-explanatory. Finds similarity, especially in Ayala's early novels.

_____. "The Progress of the Artist: A Major Theme in the Early Novels of Pérez de Ayala," *Hispanic Review*, XXVI (1958), 108-16. Title self-explanatory. Also discusses autobiographical value, and Ayala's preoccupation for Spain.

_____. "Bases de la novelística de Ramón Pérez de Ayala," *Hispania*, XLVI (1963), 57-60. Brief comment on Ayala's novelistic ideas expressed in Prologues to *Las Máscaras* and *Troteras y danzaderas*.

FERNÁNDEZ AVELLÓ, MANUEL. "Ramón Pérez de Ayala y el periodismo," *Gaceta de la Prensa Española*, 132 (Jan.-Feb., 1961), 3-13. Interesting article tracing Ayala's journalistic career.

GARCÍA MERCADAL, JOSÉ. Prologue to *Obras completas* of Pérez de Ayala (Madrid: Aguilar, 1964), I, xi-lxxv. Contains much personal information and commentaries on Ayala's life and his works in the various genres.

_____. Prologue to *Ante Azorín* by *Pérez de Ayala* (Madrid: Biblioteca Nueva, 1964), pp. 7-44. Interesting details of personal and professional nature, regarding relations between Ayala and his lifelong friend, Azorín.

HARTSOOK, JOHN H. "Literary Tradition as Form in Pérez de Ayala," *Romance Notes*, VI (1964), 21-25. Good study of Ayala's use of literary tradition as inspiration for poetry and relation between prose and this poetry in his poematic novels.

JOHNSON, ERNEST A. "The Humanities and the *Prometeo* of Ramón Pérez de Ayala," *Hispania*, XXXVIII (1955), 276-81. Very good article pointing out influences in Ayala's novel from Homer's *Odyssey* and also from Dante.

LIVINGSTONE, LEON. "The theme of the 'paradoxe sur le comédien' in the novels of Pérez de Ayala," *Hispanic Review*, XXII (1954), 208-23.

————. "Interior Duplication and the Problem of Form in the Modern Spanish Novel," *PMLA*, LXXIII (1958), 393-406. Discusses Ayala's awareness of careful form in *Belarmino y Apolonio* which he considers excellent modern example of *Quijote*-type novel. Also admires form in Ayala's poematic novels and problems of form in *El curandero de su honra*.

LONGUS. *Daphnis and Chloe*. Transl. by George Thornley (New York: Pantheon, 1949). This is the probable inspiration for Ayala's two-part novel, the story of Urbano and Simona.

LUCRETIUS, TITUS CARUS. *De rerum natura*. Eng. transl. by H. A. J. Munro (London: Bell and Daldy, 1864). Ayala states that this was the inspiration for some of his later poetry.

LUJÁN, NESTOR. Prologue to *Obras selectas* of Pérez de Ayala (Barcelona: AHR, 1957), pp. 9-27. Very good discussion of all genres of Ayala's works.

MADARIAGA, SALVADOR DE. *The Genius of Spain, and Other Essays on Contemporary Literature* (London: Oxford University Press, 1923, 2d. ed., 1930), pp. 71-86. Good interpretation of some of Ayala's novels, and special attention to his poetry. This book was translated by its author to Spanish with the title *Semblanzas literarias contemporáneas* (Barcelona: Ed. Cervantes, 1924).

MARTÍNEZ RUIZ, JOSÉ (AZORÍN). *Escritores* (Madrid: Biblioteca Nueva, 1956). This collection of earlier essays contains several on Pérez de Ayala. In the essay, "Pérez de Ayala" (pp. 79-82), Azorín notes Ayala's great sensitivity to beauty and his deep comprehension of the world. "La inteligencia y la vida" (pp. 89-94) is a favorable commentary on *Troteras y danzaderas*. In "El intelectualismo y la vida" (pp. 95-98), Azorín finds Ayala to be one of the most genuine representatives of Spanish intellectualism, and he also praises his novel, *Belarmino y Apolonio*. In "El caso prodigioso de Urbano" (pp. 107-11), Azorín comments on Urbano's strange education and subsequent success, all told in the delicate and subtle Ayalan style. Azorín is a great admirer of Pérez de Ayala and his art.

————. *Ni sí, ni no* (Barcelona: *Destino*, 1965). This volume is also a collection of earlier essays. In the first chapter, Azorín comments that the generation to which Ayala belongs has seen the problems of Spain with more precision, clarity, logic, and idealism than the writers of his own Generation of 1898. Azorín also praises Ayala's novel, *La pata de la raposa*, with its complex and subtle psychological problems. In a second chapter, "Spanish Lack of Logic," Azorín continues his commentary, concluding that this novel's lesson is that one needs more logic, more orientation, and the willful force to solve problems than the qualities possessed by Alberto, Ayala's protagonist in this early novel.

NOBLE, BETH. "The Descriptive Genius of Pérez de Ayala in *La caída de los Limones,*" *Hispania*, XL (1957), 171-75. Good commentary on Ayala's ability to portray the outer and inner reality of his characters.

ORTEGA Y GASSET, JOSÉ. *Meditaciones del Quijote* (Buenos Aires: Espasa-Calpe Argentina, 1942), pp. 13-40. In the famous opening essay addressed to the reader, Ortega explains the necessity of man's comprehending with love that which surrounds him, the circumstances through which he communicates with the universe, a doctrine very similar to that of Pérez de Ayala.

————. "Personas, Obras, Cosas," *Obras completas*, 2d ed. (Madrid: Revista de Occidente, 1950), pp. 532-35. Contains commentary on Ayala's novel *A. M. D. G.*, and expresses Ortega's complete agreement with this criticism of Jesuit education. Hopes that this book will lead to pedagogical reform in Spain.

ORTEGA, SOLEDAD. *Cartas a Galdós* (Madrid: Revista de Occidente, 1964), pp. 431-46. Señora Ortega, in editing these important missives, has included letters from Galdós to Ayala, written between 1907 and 1918, which offer valuable personal and literary information regarding these two famous writers.

NORA, EUGENIO G. DE. *La novela española contemporánea* (Madrid: Gredos, 1958), I, 467-513. A very good discussion of Ayala's novels.

REININK, K. W. *Algunos aspectos literarios y lingüísticos de la obra de Don Ramón Pérez de Ayala* (La Hague: G. B. Van Goor Zonen's U. M. N. V., 1959). A good general study of Ayala's work, his relation to the Generation of 1898, his poetic and artistic ability, and his use of Asturianisms where fitting.

RIOPÉREZ Y MILÁ, SANTIAGO. "Ramón Pérez de Ayala, otra vez poeta," *ABC*, ed. aérea, April 16, 1959. Interesting interview with Ayala, in which the great author discusses his writings, especially his poetry.

SCHRAIBMAN, JOSÉ. "Cartas inéditas de Pérez de Ayala a Galdós," *Hispanófila*, 17 (1963), 83-103. Letters contain interesting personal information. Same letters later included in book by Sebastián de la Nuez, and José Schraibman, *Cartas del archivo de Galdós* (Madrid: Taurus, 1967).

SOBEJANO, GONZALO. *Nietzsche en España* (Madrid: Gredos, 1967). Contains various references to probable influence of Nietzsche on Ayala, especially the idea of the superman.

STARKIE, WALTER. "Translator's Note," added to his English translation of *Tiger Juan* (New York: Macmillan, 1933). Various comments on Ayala and his novels, pp. 285-312.

TRENAS, JULIO. "Visita a Ramón Pérez de Ayala," *Indice*, Nos. 116-117 (Sept.-Oct. 1958), 5. Interviews in which Ayala makes interesting comments largely on poetry and genesis of his interest in theater.

URRUTIA, NORMA. De *"Troteras"* a *"Tigre Juan"—dos grandes temas de Ramón Pérez de Ayala* (Madrid: Insula, 1960). Good classification and discussion of the Ayalan novels. The "two great themes" studied are the problems of Spain and the theme of love.

VALBUENA PRAT, ANGEL. *Historia de la literatura española*, 3d ed., 3 Vols. (Barcelona: Gustavo Gili, 1950), III, 515-52. Very good study of ideology and style in novels and poetry of Ayala.

WEBER, FRANCES W. *The Literary Perspectivism of Ramón Pérez de Ayala* (Chapel Hill; The University of North Carolina Press, 1966). Interesting presentation of shifting perspective of narrator and the multiple perspectives of characters, especially in *Belarmino y Apolonio*. Studies Ayala's linguistic and narrative techniques.

Index